MATTHEW L. DAVIDSON AND VLADIMIR T. KHMELKOV

EXCELLENCE WITH INTEGRITY™

EMPLOYABILITY ESSENTIALS

21st CENTURY AND STEMCONNECTOR® 2.0 COLLEGE & CAREER READINESS

VOLUME 1

FACILITATOR GUIDE

EXCELLENCE *with* **INTEGRITY**
THE **OPTIMAL PERFORMANCE** APPROACH

Excellence with Integrity™ Employability Essentials

ISBN-13:978-1-940-77010-9

CONTENTS

Dear DMACC Student:

I am pleased to introduce <u>Employability Essentials</u>, a result of a collaborative initiative called LE@D – Leadership Excellence at DMACC, led by a dedicated group of professionals from The Robert D. and Billie Ray Center, Des Moines Area Community College, and the Institute for Excellence & Ethics.

The purpose of this initiative was to develop a pilot program that will infuse core leadership competencies needed for your success as a college student, helping to ensure that you're ready for your career and effective in the workplace.

There is a convergence of evidence indicating that the development of core competencies and skills is critical for education and economic vitality in the U.S. For example, the report *Are They Really Ready to Work* describes survey data from several hundred employers in which the authors conclude that "when basic knowledge and applied skills rankings are combined for each educational level, the top five 'most important' are always applied skills," with work ethic and professionalism at the top of the list (2006, p. 10). When asked to rate the importance of work ethic and professionalism, approximately 80 percent indicated it was very important for high school graduates, approximately 83 percent reported it was very important for two-year college and tech school graduates, and approximately 94 percent reported it was very important for four-year college graduates (2006, p. 20).

<u>Employability Essentials</u> provides you with an opportunity to develop skills that have not traditionally been offered and aligned with your specific program content. I commend you for embracing this opportunity and encourage you to apply these learning experiences at every opportunity. By doing so, you will distinguish yourself as a qualified, well-prepared learner and employee.

All my best,

MD Isley, M.S.
Dean - Business, Management and Information Technology
Des Moines Area Community College

Ankeny Campus   Boone Campus   Carroll Campus   Newton Campus   Urban Campus   West Campus
2006 S. Ankeny Blvd   1125 Hancock Drive   906 N. Grant Road   600 N. 2nd Avenue W   1100 7th Street   5959 Grand Avenue
Ankeny, IA 50023-3993 Boone, IA 50036-5399 Carroll, IA 51401-2525 Newton, IA 50208-3049 Des Moines, IA 50314-2597 W. Des Moines, IA 50266-5302
515-964-6200   515-432-7203   712-792-1755   641-791-3622   515-244-4226   515-633-2407

Introduction

Development of competencies that are at the core of excellence, integrity, and professionalism remains critical for economic vitality in the U.S. For example, the report *Pathways to Prosperity* (2011) argues that "within the U.S. economy….many adults lack the skills and work ethic needed for many jobs that pay a middle-class wage." Summarizing data from several hundred employers, the report *Are They Really Ready to Work* concludes that "when basic knowledge and applied skills rankings are combined for each educational level, the top five 'most important' are always applied skills," with work ethic and professionalism at the top of the list (2006, p. 10). When asked to rate the importance of work ethic and professionalism, about 80% of the employers indicated it was very important for high school graduates, 83% reported is was very important for two-year college and tech school graduates, and 94% said it was very important for four-year college graduates (2006, p. 20).

The *Excellence with Integrity* Series targets a set of essential skills demonstrated in the research to be vital for success in school, sport, work, and life. The series feature replicable teaching and learning strategies presented in the form of Excellence with Integrity™ tools. IEE tools are based on cutting-edge research and act as the core of each introductory lesson, as well as guides and standards for continued learning beyond the initial experience.

We have worked hard to make the teaching and learning resources in this series practitioner-friendly for implementation. Yet, effective implementation ultimately requires you to work hard to make any curricular resource, including this one, fit you and your teaching style, as well as your students' developmental level, learning styles, etc. for an optimal learning experience.

How deep and enduring the impact of this curriculum will be depends in large part on how it is implemented. To be effective, use of these materials requires preparation before implementing, monitoring while implementing, and reflection after implementing.

So, in order to maximize the quality of the experience we suggest you take a few minutes to familiarize yourself with the overall design and specific implementation insights for making the most of the resources in this book.

Overview of Excellence with Integrity Series

The Excellence with Integrity series targets specific skills and competencies identified by IEE as essential competencies (see "Excellence with Integrity™ Competencies" on page xiv). These competencies are aligned with the 21st Century Skills framework, as well as two of the capability platforms of STEM2.0.

Classroom Instructional Resources

The ***Facilitator Guide*** consists of learning modules, with each module designed to provide introductory experience to a particular competency or learning target. The whole module can be delivered as one lesson, broken over several classes, or modified for delivery in any other way that would best fit the learning environment.

Structurally, each learning module includes three major components:

1. Objective, Overview, Preparation and Materials list.
2. Delivery Steps:
    a) Introduction.
    b) Guided Practice.
    c) Closure & Assessment.
3. Extensions.

The instructions and activities presented in the Facilitator Guide are intended to show one possible way of introducing the knowledge about the targeted skill or competency; it is the job of the facilitator to select what would work best for their audience, and for the environment, context, and time in which the module content will be delivered.

Matching ***Student Workbooks*** include

a) the learning activities that students engage in during the introductory experience in class,

b) the Excellence with Integrity™ Tools that they can continue using as they work on the extensions,

c) rubrics and space for reflection and planning.

Conceptually, each learning module incorporates two main features:

• research-based tool(s)—visual summary of the essential knowledge and/or replicable skill development process, and

• an experiential introduction to the tool(s)—guided practice.

The research-based tools represent the distillation of the relevant academic, experimental, and field research into a teaching strategy, process, checklist, or rubric. In each module the learner is introduced to a strategy, and then has a chance to experience it through simulated activities.

The skills that are introduced in a module become stable habits when they are consistently and pervasively learned, practiced, refined, and reinforced. When the habits of individuals (students and instructors) become the shared way of behaving for the group, then the new group habits become part of the overall culture.

In sum, competencies identify *what* we want students to be able to do, whereas the teaching and learning tools provide a guide for development of habits of the mind, heart, and hand—*how* we want students to learn and act.

Following the introductory experience, Extensions suggest a few additional opportunities to practice the skill after the introductory lesson using the lesson tool(s) as guides for behavior. The extensions provided are just a sample of unlimited opportunities for integration of skill development into different situations and contexts outside of and beyond the initial lesson that you and your students can tap into.

Transition to Learning Through Real-Life Experiences

The third resources in the Excellence with Integrity series allows extending the development of the Excellence with Integrity skills further into internships, on-the-job trainings, and similar practicum-type experiences.

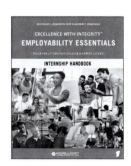

The **Internship Handbook** targets the skills and competencies introduced in the classroom environment. Each module includes:

a) review of the core knowledge about targeted competencies summarized in a professional journal article format, with links to relevant videos, articles, or books for engaging and expanded learning;

b) Excellence with Integrity™ Tools, and

c) Optimal Performance™ Assessment & Development tools and strategies for self-reflection, coaching, and feedback on the real-world implementation of the targeted skills.

Optimal Performance™ Assessment & Development

Forget Perfect; Find Optimal

No individual would be expected to be equally proficient in all skills, or to implement them with equal effectiveness in every circumstance or situation. IEE's Optimal Performance approach recognizes that nobody is perfect and that each person has different strengths and weaknesses, and that we all struggle at times in our quest to put the organizational values and expectation into action amid the real-world challenges.

Optimal performance avoids EXCESS or DEFICIENCY relative to:

(1) the organizational *mission* and *vision*, *goals* and *expectations*,

(2) each person's *sensibilities* and *capabilities*, and

(3) the real-world *circumstances* faced in one's career or the life of the organization.

DEFICIENT	**OPTIMAL**	**EXCESSIVE**
TOO LITTLE	Just right for desired goals,	TOO MUCH
Detracts/Prevents Growth	person, & circumstances	Detracts/Prevents Growth

Optimal Performance Self-Studies built by IEE are standardized formative assessment and development tools. They capture what the targeted competencies and expectations should look like, sound like, and feel like in practice.

Each self-study includes a set of items identifying a range of behaviors and practices for each of the corresponding competency. These are most typical types of behaviors and practices that apply across organizations or contexts.

Trainees/mentees achieve optimal performance when they implement these behaviors and practices consistently, intentionally, and in a way that matches expectations, specific circumstances, and an individual's capabilities. Leaders and/or mentors ensure consistency in formation of trainees' attitudes toward work, developing their core skills, and shaping the overall culture of excellence by making Optimal Performance standardized assessment and development tools the central element of their leadership or mentoring.

4 KEYS: Research-Based Instructional Strategies

The Optimal Performance Assessment and Development Process is based on IEE's framework of four essential instructional practices that help ensure growth in individuals and organizations. They are "keys" because when utilized strategically they "unlock" transformational insight and sustainable growth experiences. The 4 KEYS are Self-Study, Other-Study, Support & Challenge, and Performance/Simulation.

⊘ *EXCELLENCE WITH INTEGRITY*

4 KEYS
RESEARCH-BASED MASTER STRATEGIES

Self-Study:
Self-reflection to identify strengths and areas for improvement, to examine beliefs and experiences, to set goals, monitor progress, and revise as needed.

Other-Study:
The study of people, products, and performances to identify positive and productive behaviors, practices, and habits to emulate — and negative or ineffective examples to avoid.

Support & Challenge:
Intentional efforts to establish safety and trust, to set shared norms, to enhance personal and collective responsibility, and to provide encouragement, expertise, and accountability.

Performance/Simulation:
Opportunities to enhance confidence and expertise by engaging in or simulating real life experiences through deliberate practice, experiential learning and authentic assessment.

Adapted from Lickona & Davidson (2005).

　　　　www.excellenceandethics.org

Why Self-Study?

Optimal Performance Self-Studies are essential tools facilitating trainees' growth. They can be utilized by trainees on their own, independent of mentor, coach, or manager input, as they reflect on their past performance and look for ways to improve.

Part 1 of the Self-Study asks the trainee to reflect on their performance over a certain period of time and rate it from *Inadequate* to *Optimal*. The standardized items help trainees focus on the important concrete aspects of the behavioral expectations for each targeted competency or goal. In doing so, trainees gain clarity about the norms and expectations, and their ability to meet them.

Ways to maximize effectiveness of the self-study:

1. Starting with the time period of focus is important. Whatever we choose to establish as the time period, that's what is under reflection. The past six days, or six weeks or six years? It makes no difference, except for clearly anchoring the reflection. We need to be clear and consistent about the time period.

2. Clarity about the time period helps clarify our benchmarks. First, specific expectations may vary due to business cycles or change in our role within the organization. Second, the circumstances of this time period, such as multiple external factors and events, are important. Complete turmoil and uncertainty or smooth sailing? Once again, neither are bad or good per se, but we should be fair in our assessment of our performance. We need to reflect in our assessment on both the specific expectations and the specific circumstances.

3. The individual capabilities and sensibilities make up another benchmark. The goal is that everyone be a work in progress in trying to optimally implement the targeted competencies and expectations, while allowing for the fact that we each have things that come to us either more easily or with greater difficulty. We need to acknowledge our strengths, and we need to be honest with ourselves in recognizing and rating accordingly items that require further focus and improvement.

What's working? What should be done better or differently?

Part 2 asks the trainee to conduct the next, more in-depth level of Self-Study. Question 1 asks to identify examples when the way they put the competency into action was in their estimation optimal or close to optimal. Reflecting on this question, trainees make their understanding of what is optimal more concrete and specific.

This process helps trainees build up their confidence and sense of pride for their capabilities (e.g., "I struggle with conflict and I've got many examples where I fall short of the optimal, but in these instances I was pretty close to optimal."). When earned through real and concrete examples, self-esteem is a powerful psychological factor leading to a strong positive attitude toward the future.

Many—if not all—of the most important skills (such as communication, time management, collaboration, leadership) require positive attitude. But they also need vigilant and persistent effort, an intentional focus on seeking out ways to get better. When we fall short of optimal this doesn't necessarily mean we're a bad person—it may simply mean we have high expectations and some challenging circumstances. The important question to ask and answer for both attitude and effort is: *what do we intend to do better or differently?*

Question 2 in Part 2 prompts trainees to come up with action steps for what they can do **better or differently** in the future to put the competency into action in a *more* optimal way. This section is an opportunity for trainees to plan for growth and goal achievement. They can start by identifying specific things they need to do differently or better. They need then to plan for deliberate practice—ways in which they intend to improve their knowledge or skills. They also need to plan for ways to get the external support and expertise.

For a mentor, coach, or leader, this is a key section for determining and shaping trainees' true self-knowledge. Does their understanding of what caused less-than-optimal performance make sense? Is it thorough and accurate? Does their plan for ensuring optimal performance in the future make sense? Is it real and meaningful?

Thus, the Optimal Performance Self-Studies integrate *assessment* of past performance with *development* toward future growth and improvement. In addition, when utilized as part of a formal or informal goal achievement process, the Optimal Performance Self-Studies may serve as practical tools for *Measuring, Monitoring, and Revising* one's goal achievement plan (see Goal Achievement tool in Module 1.1).

Mentoring: Other-Study plus Support & Challenge

Optimal Performance Self-Studies are most effective when used in conjunction with feedback provided to the individual by a mentor, coach, or manager — a 180-degree assessment and development process. By filling out the same form as used by their mentee and reflecting on the mentee in doing so, and then sharing and discussing it with the mentee, mentors provide the *Support & Challenge* essential for personal growth and improvement.

Ways to maximize effectiveness of the Optimal Performance process in mentoring:

1. Feedback from mentors needs to include both *praise* and *polish*: praising the mentee's successes and improvement helps build up morale, whereas challenging to do certain things better ensures focus on excellence.

2. Reflections about what to do better or differently are greatly enhanced when self-studies are accompanied by *Other-Study* examples. Mentors can strengthen the feedback process by providing additional definitions, indicators, and examples of what the target value or competency looks, sounds, and feels like in action. They can use examples from across the organization, from their own experiences, or from "aspirational" or "model" individuals or organizations. Other-studies can also include examples of behaviors to avoid.

3. *Excellence with Integrity Tools* can be used as guides for targeted behaviors or practices. E&E Tools are in essence checklists that condense theory and research into a set of concrete steps or actions that can be followed for improvement.

4. Feedback should not be general in nature, as in "You should improve communication." Mentor suggestions for improvement must focus on *specific* changes and improvements (such as, for example, "You can improve communication by asking questions that verify and clarify; by using "I"-statements and avoiding "You"-statements."). Mentor insights need also include sugges-

tions for ***deliberate practice*** around particular skills targeted for improvement.

The best coaches and mentors thrive because they avoid destructive attacks of the person, and instead focus specifically on the instructions of what to do better or differently and why. They *name it* ("take a look at this particular idea or behavior or skill..."); they *frame it* ("when facing this particular circumstance or situation..."); they *explain it* ("it must be done *this* way, not *that* way, because..."); and they *practice it*.

In sum, the Optimal Performance Assessment and Development Process incorporates consistent ***Self-Study*** of optimal performance behaviors and trainees' action plans toward meeting their goals. ***Support & Challenge*** from mentors ensures accountability and expertise, enhanced by ***Other-Study*** models of what and how to do better or differently. Ultimately, optimal performance is achieved via trainee's deliberate practice (***Performance/Simulation***) within the real-world circumstances focused on concrete and significant improvement.

Work Ethic, Goal Achievement, Problem Solving, Innovation

Committing to high standards and continuous improvement through work ethic, self-management, and goal achievement

- Adhere to strong internal standards of excellence.
- Exhibit perseverance and self-motivation when things are not easy.
- Exhibit the positive attitude and persistent effort needed to continuously improve.
- Seek external support and incorporate feedback effectively.
- Develop, monitor, and modify goal achievement action steps.

Exhibiting critical thinking, problem solving, creativity and innovation

- Maximize the potential of available resources.
- Consider different perspectives, approaches, and possibilities when solving problems.
- Leverage individual and collective strengths to overcome performance challenges.
- Utilize effective decision-making across diverse social and professional contexts and situations.

Communication, Collaboration, Negotiation, Teamwork

Communicating and collaborating with efficiency and effectiveness

- Clarify and verify understanding.
- Express views and ideas effectively.
- Use effective communication strategies in diverse contexts, settings and situations.
- Recognize and respond to the feelings and perspectives of others.

Developing teamwork through positive and productive relationships

- Adapt to new roles and changing strategy in the pursuit of a team goal.
- Exercise flexibility and willingness to make necessary compromises to accomplish a common goal.
- Recognize and balance diverse beliefs and perspectives to reach effective solutions.
- Work efficiently and effectively with others.

EXCELLENCE WITH INTEGRITY™ COMPETENCIES

Priority & Stress Management, Growth, Life Purpose

Managing priorities and time, managing and reducing stress

- Identify factors that contribute to (drivers) or detract from (preventers) effective time management.
- Organize, prioritize, plan and execute tasks effectively.
- Implement productive strategies for reducing stress.
- Use failures, disappointments, and setbacks as opportunities to learn and improve.
- Know how and when to ask for help.

Living a purposeful, balanced and healthy life

- Pursue multidimensional life-goals, interests, and aspirations.
- Work to develop personal strengths and overcome personal challenges.
- Live a safe, balanced, and healthy life.

Integrity, Responsibility, Leadership, Service

Demonstrating emotional intelligence, integrity, and responsibility

- Demonstrate ethical conscience and competence.
- Exhibit personal accountability for responsibilities and obligations.
- Act with integrity according to a well-formed ethical code of conduct.
- Hold self and others accountable.

Leading and serving others

- Use one's talents and skills to serve the good of the group/team.
- Use interpersonal and group management skills to lead others effectively.
- Motivate and empower others.
- Commit to shared goals and the collective good.

1. From Goal Setting to Goal Achievement

Module 1-1: Goal Achievement Process

Competency: Benchmark current state (baseline starting point) and desired state (end goal)

Tools: *Goal Achievement Process*

Objective

Students will use the Goal Achievement Process to develop the skills required for effective and efficient goal achievement.

Overview

1. Students will engage in a Self-Study to identify feelings and emotions associated with feeling lost or misguided.

2. Students will view an Other-Study video of Michael Stewart, *GED Success Story*, and identify examples of the Goal Achievement Process in action.

3. Students will work in small groups to create and perform a "how-to" presentation on the use of the Goal Achievement Process. As part of the activity introduction, students will view the Other-Study video, *How to Get on American Idol*, as a model for the "how-to" presentation.

Preparation

1. Determine how you will establish the behavioral norms needed to ensure a positive and productive learning experience for all students.

2. Determine how much time will be allotted to create the "how-to" presentations and the procedures for delivering and judging the presentation.

3. Prepare external streaming video content:

   a. Review IEE policy regarding use of external content.

   b. Michael Stewart, "GED Success Story"

      https://www.youtube.com/watch?v=vN9rOIaRYC0

   c. "How to Get on American Idol"

      http://www.youtube.com/watch?v=-hGAIE5cnpY.

Materials

- Materials for students to use in the "how-to" presentation.

Module Delivery Steps

Introduction:

1. Begin with the Self-Study in #1 in the Student Workbook. It includes a scenario describing a situation where one is lost in the woods. Have students discuss the prompt in #1 with a partner.

2. Continue with a whole-class discussion about the thoughts and feelings identified by students with their partners. Talking points may include:

    ◊   *Mind racing. Adrenaline pumping. Mentally retracing your steps. Second-guessing every move you made that got you to this point.*

    ◊   *Scared. Frustrated. Angry. Overwhelmed. Completely distressed and absolutely ready to hit the panic button.*

    ◊   *These are just some of the thoughts and feelings you might have described as you considered how you would handle being lost in the woods.*

    ◊   *You may never have been or ever will be lost in the woods. And yet frequently, as we try to make our way through life, we feel lost.*

    ◊   *If you've ever felt unsure about how you ended up in your current situation, if you've been unsure about what direction to turn to get out, if you've ever felt like you're going in circles and not making progress, then you know what it feels like to be lost.*

3. Display and introduce the Goal Achievement Process. Introduction to the tool may sound something like this:

    ◊   *Goal achievement is essentially a process of figuring out "How do WE get from here to there?".*

    ◊   *Usually when we think of goals, we think about setting them. It is important to identify goals that matter to us (i.e., **set** our goals), but we also need to figure out what it takes to **achieve** our goals. How do we get from where we are now to where we want to be in the future?*

    ◊   *Sometimes we know the exact way from point A to point B. But often getting from where we are currently to where we want to be in life is uncertain, and therefore difficult and confusing, and we may experience many of the same thoughts and feelings as though we were lost in the woods.*

◊ For centuries people have been developing different tools to help us navigate our way from here to there. Early travelers used the stars as a navigation guide. Explorers developed detailed maps, so that others could follow their paths. Today, GPS devices, or Global Positioning Systems, help guide us from here to there.

◊ GPS navigation starts with two simple but essential questions: What is your current location? What is your desired destination? In other words: Where are you? And where do you want to go? The GPS system then develops a step-by-step (or, turn-by-turn) plan that you follow to get from your starting point to your end goal. As you make progress along the route, GPS navigation monitors your progress and assists with detours and course-corrections as obstacles or deviations come up.

◊ The Goal Achievement Process is designed to help you navigate your progress towards your goals with a similar logic.

>> *First, no matter what you are trying to achieve, no matter what challenge you are trying to overcome, you need to start by figuring out your current position (or starting point) and your desired destination (or end goal). Then you need to plot the action steps to get you from your starting point to your end goal.*

>> *Second, once the plan is in place and you begin to put it into action, the Goal Achievement Process encourages you to regularly measure and monitor where you are, and to revise your plan (or your action steps) as needed. This is one of the most important differences between goal setting and the Goal Achievement Process. It is not sufficient to set goals and make a plan: achieving your goals requires that you continuously measure and monitor your progress to see what changes may need to be made along the way.*

>> *Finally, the "how do **WE** get from here to there" Goal Achievement Process also asks you to consider who is traveling with you and how they will help you, as you try to get from your current position to your desired goal. These won't always be the same individuals. Depending on your goal, your companions on your journey may change (or you may have different companions for different aspects of your journey). But, at every step, you need to be proactive to seek support and challenge from individuals who are able to provide you with expertise, accountability, and encouragement that you will need to make progress.*

4. Continue the lesson with an Other-Study video about Michael Stewart (#2 in the Student Workbook).

YouTube video of Michael Stewart - GED Success Story

https://www.youtube.com/watch?v=vN9rOIaRYC0

5. Facilitate a discussion to debrief components of the Goal Achievement Process that students identified in the video.

Possible examples:

Current location: Detention facility/Re-entry facility, lost, no idea what to do with his life.

Support and Challenge: woman at re-entry facility provided guidance, family and friends did not provide support or positive influence.

Action Steps: GED would open up opportunities; had to learn to be organized and divide time between work and school.

Measure & Monitor. Revise as Needed: earned GED, set new desired location — welding program, a step towards getting a job working on wind turbines.

Guided Practice:

6. Divide the students into small groups for the main learning activity.

7. Explain that students will create a "how-to" presentation which will explain and demonstrate how to use the Goal Achievement Process. Each group will share their "how-to" presentation with the entire class. The class will evaluate each presentation using the Goal Achievement Process and the GAP Presentation Criteria shown in #3 in the Student Workbook. Start by reviewing the Criteria rubric.

8. Use the Other-Study video, "How to Get on American Idol", to set the stage for this activity. Ask students to use the GAP Presentation Criteria to evaluate the effectiveness of the video.

    http://www.youtube.com/watch?v=-hGAIE5cnpY

9. Facilitate a discussion among students about their other-study observations. Clarify any misinterpretations of the GAP Presentation Criteria that may come up during the discussion.

10. Give groups ample time to prepare their "how-to" presentations.

11. Have each group share their presentation. Have other students take notes about each presentation.

12. Facilitate a debrief allowing each group to receive feedback on their "how-to" presentation.

Closure & Assessment:

13.   Close the lesson by reiterating and discussing the value of the Goal Achievement Process. Leave the students with final thoughts which may include the following quote:

    ◊   *When we feel lost or unsure about where we are going, it can be difficult to see the way out. But, it's important to remember that* ***"the journey of a thousand miles begins with a first step."*** *- Confucius*

Extension:

14.   **Other-Study:** Have students interview their peers or an adult to discover how they set and monitor their goals. As part of the interview, have students use the Goal Achievement Process as a guide for their questioning. Following the interview, have students reflect and share their experiences through writing and discussion opportunities.

15.   **Self-Study:** Provide students opportunities to use the Goal Achievement Process and reflect on what components of the process they feel proficient using and which components aren't as fluid or natural for them to use.

16.   **Performance/Simulation:** As students have opportunities to use and reflect on the Goal Achievement Process, facilitate discussions and allow students to share their experiences and levels of implementation. Encourage a culture of constructive critique which is focused on using the tool to its full extent.

17.   **Support & Challenge:** Have students create a poster that illustrates what support and challenge looks like and sounds like from various people, e.g., peers, teachers, parents, employers, counselors, etc., in relation to the Goal Achievement Process. Encourage students to be specific in their depictions. Ask students to share their posters with individuals outside the class and get feedback on them.

Planning and Reflection

Module 1-2: Goal Mapping

Competency: Balance tactical (short-term) and strategic (long-term) goals

Tools: *Goal Map & Goal Map Checklist*

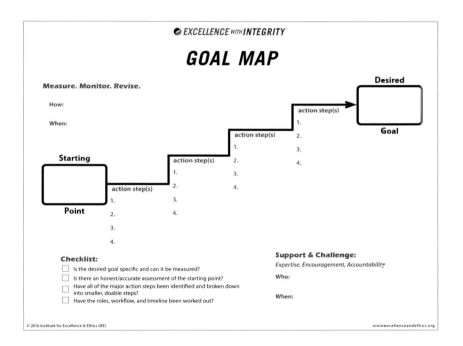

Objective

Students will use the Goal Map to map a personal goal.

Overview

1. Students will work on completion of a goal map based on the Liz Murray video clip.

2. Students will select a personal goal and create a goal map for the identified goal.

3. Students will work in partnerships using the Goal Map Checklist to verify the strength of their individual goal maps.

Preparation

1. Determine how you will establish the behavioral norms needed to ensure a positive and productive learning experience for all students.

2. Determine the amount of time you will allot for students to complete the goal map for the Liz Murray Other-Study.

3. Determine how much time will be allotted for the students to create their individual goal maps.

4. Determine the procedure and time that will be allotted for students to use the Goal Map Checklist to verify the strength of their completed Goal Maps.

5. Prepare external streaming video content:

   a. Review IEE policy regarding use of external content.

   b. Ms. Ochs

      http://www.nbcnews.com/id/21134540/vp/18351140#18351140

   c. Liz Murray:

      Part 1: Growing Up

      http://www.youtube.com/watch?v=hScKkr5nxlI

      Part 2: The Serenity Coin

      http://www.youtube.com/watch?v=q72CU-jJZ-A

      Part 3: Making Choices

      http://www.youtube.com/watch?v=O8H_i22_9hc.

Module Delivery Steps

Introduction:

1. Begin by having students read the quote by Diana Scharf Hunt: "*Goals are dreams with deadlines*" and discuss with a partner how it applies to their lives (#1 in the Student Workbook).

2. Facilitate a whole-class discussion of the meaning of the quote and how it applies to students' own life.

3. Facilitate the Other-Study of Ms. Ochs who achieved her personal goal of graduating college at the age of 95.

    http://www.nbcnews.com/id/21134540/vp/18351140#18351140

4. Introduce the Goal Map. Introduction to the tools might go something like this:

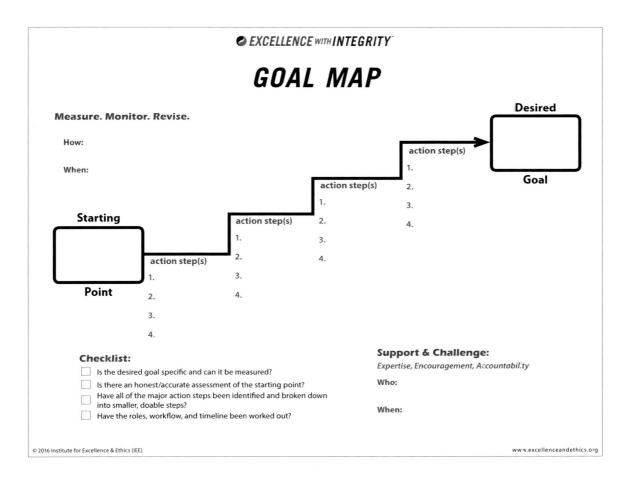

◊ *Usually when we think of goals, we think about setting them. But by itself setting goals is not enough; we want to figure out what it takes to achieve the goals that we set for ourselves. How do we get from where we are now to where we want to be in the near future?*

◊ *We do this by creating a map consisting of action steps that would take us towards our goals. Our action steps are the things most in our control.*

◊ *Once we've created a Goal Map, we want to check to make sure it is as strong as it can be by using the following Checklist.*

» *First, we should be sure that the desired goal we're going after is specific and measurable.*

» *Second, we must be sure that we have an accurate understanding of our current position. If we know where we're starting from, no matter how bad it might seem, we can create a detailed plan of action. If we are not honest or accurate, we will ignore or miss out on key action steps that are needed.*

» *With a specific end-goal and a clear starting position, we need to make sure we have identified the major action steps required, and that we have broken them down into doable, smaller steps with a concrete timeline for each.*

» *Finally, we need to identify who will support and challenge us: what the roles would be for people on our 'team', when and how would we work together, and what our timeline would be.*

Guided Practice:

5. Break students into partnerships for the first part of the guided practice.

6. Begin the guided practice by showing students the Other-Study video(s) of Liz Murray. Determine whether you will use all 3 clips or only one of them. (If you only have time for one, Part 2 may be the best to use.) Instruct students to watch carefully, so that they will be able to work with their groups to construct a Goal Map that may have been used by Liz Murray in her quest to move from homeless to Harvard. Introduction to this video clip may sound something like this:

◊ *Liz Murray was a seventeen-year-old lost within the confines of her life. She had to face the reality that she was homeless and living on the streets of New York City. But the key to her turnaround was not just understanding her current position in life. Her turnaround came when she considered what she really wanted from life. She found the path out of her current situation by setting a goal to get a college education. Once she knew where she was and where she wanted to be, she just needed to work hard to plan and execute the action steps needed to realize her goal.*

◊ *Homeless to Harvard sounds easy, but realizing that dream obviously required detailed action steps. After watching the video(s), let's see if we can use a goal map to navigate her course of action.*

Growing Up

http://www.youtube.com/watch?v=hScKkr5nxlI

The Serenity Coin

http://www.youtube.com/watch?v=q72CU-jJZ-A

Making Choices

http://www.youtube.com/watch?v=O8H_i22_9hc

7.   After watching the video(s), allow students time to complete the goal map in #2 in the Student Workbook. Introduction to the activity may sound something like this:

◊ *There were at least four major action steps Liz needed to go from homeless to Harvard. (1) She needed to secure food & shelter, (2) graduate from high school, (3) apply and get accepted to Harvard, and (4) find a way to pay for going to Harvard.*

◊ *Each of these four major action steps was likely made up of a number of smaller steps. For example, securing food and shelter probably required that she call friends or local shelters to find a place to live. She needed to get money (probably by getting a part-time job), get food, and clean clothes for school.*

◊ *With your group, work to fill in the other parts of the Goal Map Liz Murray may have used. Use the model provided for the action step "secure food and shelter" to help you get started.*

8.   After a reasonable time has been allotted for the construction of the goal map, conduct a group discussion on the completion of Liz Murray's Goal Map. Possible points may include:

◊ *As you broke the four major action steps down, different groups might have come up with somewhat different small action steps. You also may have started to think about other major action steps outside of the four provided examples.*

◊ *However, what should be clear from this task is that achieving a goal as big as going from homeless to Harvard takes a lot of smaller action steps.*

◊ *By itself, setting the goal didn't get Liz Murray to Harvard. Rather, she realized her dream by breaking her overall goal down into manageable steps. Then she worked hard on the things within her control.*

9. Continue by explaining to students that the next part of the lesson is to apply the Goal Map to their own life. Students will work independently to select a goal they would like to achieve and work to create a goal map (#3 in the Student Workbook).

10. After students have completed their Goal Map, allow time to use the Goal Map Checklist to check the strength of their Goal Maps (#4 in the Student Workbook). Start by having students review the Goal Maps of their partner, paying specific attention to any sections in which the partner has checked "unsure."

11. Then, have students return the goal maps to their authors. Encourage students to reflect upon their own goal maps and give themselves an overall score using the grading system provided in #5 in the Student Workbook.

Closure & Assessment:

12. Close the lesson by reiterating the usefulness of the Goal Map and reviewing the components of the process:

    » *Create a goal map to mark your starting point and identify your desired destination.*

    » *Write down the major action steps required to get you to your goal, and break those down into smaller, doable steps.*

    » *Measure and monitor your progress, and revise as needed.*

    » *Seek support and challenge from individuals who can provide you with expertise, accountability, and encouragement.*

Extension:

13. **Other-Study:** Have students identify Other-Study examples of people that have worked hard to achieve their goals. Allow students to share examples they find with the class. Then, as a group, use the Goal Map to reflect on the process and action steps taken to achieve the indicated goal.

14. **Self-Study:** Have students keep a journal in which they reflect on the progress they are making with the goal they have mapped. Encourage students to be open and honest in their reflections. At the end of an assigned period of time (1 week, 2 weeks, etc.), give students an opportunity to read back over their journal entries and reflect on them collectively in some way (written response, partner or group sharing, one-on-one meetings with you, etc.).

15. **Performance/Simulation:** Have students continue working with the Goal Map by allowing them to present the process and personally selected other-study examples to their peers. Encourage students to have several examples, as well as several completed goal maps, to work with peers, as they extend their understanding to others.

16. **Support & Challenge:** Have students update a partner, a small group, or the entire class on the progress they are making in achieving their goal. Give students an opportunity to check back in at regular intervals (every day, every few days, once per week, etc.) to see if they are sticking with the action steps they identified. Encourage students to be open and honest, using check-ins as opportunities for continued growth.

Planning and Reflection

EMPLOYABILITY ESSENTIALS FACILITATOR GUIDE

Module 1-3: Attitude + Effort = Improvement

Competency: Develop the attitude and effort needed to revise and continuously improve

Tools: *AEI Rubric*

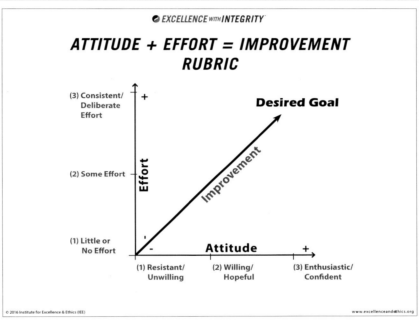

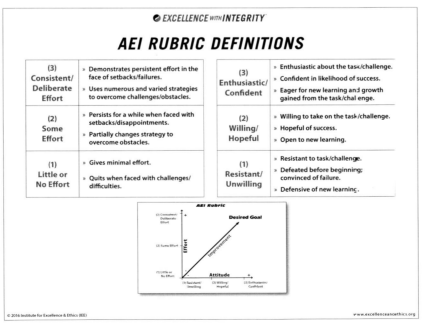

Objective

Students will use the Attitude-Effort-Improvement Rubric to understand, develop and monitor the factors that contribute to growth and improvement.

Overview

1. The class will engage in a discussion regarding their responses to a disappointing situation.

2. The students will view Other-Study videos and work in small groups to identify the components of the Attitude-Effort-Improvement rubric.

3. Students will work in small groups to complete fishbone diagrams on the drivers and preventers that contribute to, or detract from, positive attitude and strong effort.

Preparation

1. Determine how you will establish the behavioral norms needed to ensure a positive and productive learning experience for all students.

2. Choose an Other-Study video or videos you will use.

3. Determine the amount of time students will have to complete the fishbone diagrams.

4. Prepare external streaming video content:

    a. Review IEE policy regarding use of external content.

    b. The Patrick Willis Story:
       http://www.youtube.com/watch?v=uN22zvvxAJ0

    c. The Ben Comen Story:
       http://www.youtube.com/watch?v=hZtNbUhr6qQ

    d. Michael Jordan - Maybe It's My Fault:

       http://www.youtube.com/watch?v=_-EyRUgp9Mk

Module Delivery Steps

Introduction:

1. Begin with #1 in the Student Workbook:

    ◊ *Consider the following:*

    Although you set a goal of getting a B in an important class, you just got your first test back worth 30% of your final grade, unfortunately you got a D. If you were in this situation, what is your response? Are you:

    a. *Disappointed but determined*
    b. *Disappointed and doubting*
    c. *Disappointed, discouraged, and done trying!*

2. Facilitate a whole-class discussion by asking students to share and explain their response. Key points to wrap up the discussion may include:

    ◊ *Everybody responds differently when they are faced with challenges like the one presented, but would you believe that the response you choose provides powerful insights into your long-term success?*

    ◊ *University of Kansas Psychologist C.R. Snyder actually used the same question about getting a D on an important exam that you just discussed to compare the academic achievement of students with high and low hope.*

    ◊ *Snyder found that hope, or what we call positive attitude, was in fact a better predictor of first semester grades of college freshmen than were their ACT scores.*

    ◊ *Snyder's research found that students with a positive attitude set higher goals.*

    Source: Daniel Goleman. (1995). *Emotional Intelligence: Why it can matter more than IQ.* New York: Bantam Books.

3. Display and introduce the Attitude-Effort-Improvement Rubric. Introduction to the tool may sound something like this:

    ◊ *The Attitude-Effort-Improvement (AEI) Rubric summarizes research on achievement in a simple formula for success: Attitude + Effort = Improvement.*

◊ The tool offers two 3-point rubrics that provide clear benchmarks for communicating, measuring and monitoring.

◊ AEI is a simple formula, but not necessarily easy. It doesn't promise that you will reach your goals overnight, nor does it promise that you're going to achieve at the same level as someone else.

◊ AEI says, of all the things within your control, attitude and effort are two of the most powerful factors leading to growth and improvement.

◊ Research has established that given roughly the same abilities, attitude and effort make all the difference in predicting improvement and achievement.

◊ Positive attitude and effort lead to high levels of improvement and overall achievement.

◊ Poor attitude and low effort lead to little or no improvement and lower levels in overall achievement.

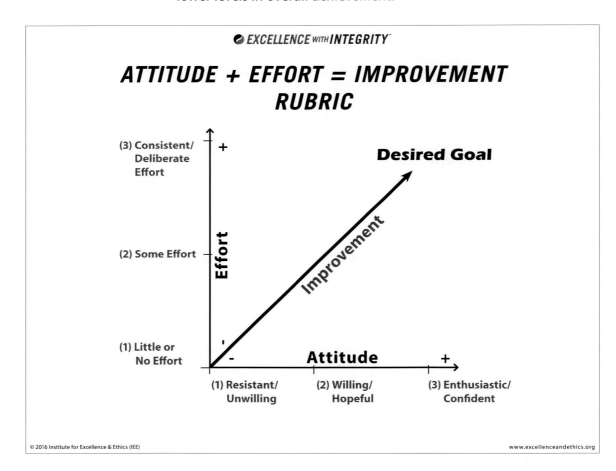

● EXCELLENCE WITH INTEGRITY

ATTITUDE + EFFORT = IMPROVEMENT RUBRIC

© 2016 Institute for Excellence & Ethics (IEE)   www.excellenceandethics.org

● EXCELLENCE WITH INTEGRITY

AEI RUBRIC DEFINITIONS

(3) Consistent/ Deliberate Effort	» Demonstrates persistent effort in the face of setbacks/failures. » Uses numerous and varied strategies to overcome challenges/obstacles.	(3) Enthusiastic/ Confident	» Enthusiastic about the task/challenge. » Confident in likelihood of success. » Eager for new learning and growth gained from the task/challenge.
(2) Some Effort	» Persists for a while when faced with setbacks/disappointments. » Partially changes strategy to overcome obstacles.	(2) Willing/ Hopeful	» Willing to take on the task/challenge. » Hopeful of success. » Open to new learning.
(1) Little or No Effort	» Gives minimal effort. » Quits when faced with challenges/ difficulties.	(1) Resistant/ Unwilling	» Resistant to task/challenge. » Defeated before beginning; convinced of failure. » Defensive of new learning.

AEI Rubric

www.excellenceandethics.org

Guided Practice:

4.   Divide the class into small groups for the main learning activities.

5.   Facilitate one or more Other-Studies from the options below or use your own examples.

Choose from the Other-Study options:

A. The Patrick Willis Story:

http://www.youtube.com/watch?v=uN22zvvxAJ0

Patrick Willis is one of the top 10 football players in the NFL. When in high school, his brothers and sisters were removed from the home of their biological father and taken in by one of the coaches in order to avoid moving 85 miles away. The story highlights how Patrick's attitude and effort help keep his siblings together, as well as achieve his personal goals in life. The Other-Study video is 10:00 minutes in length; however, the last 2:30 are highlights of Patrick's college and professional career.

B. The Ben Comen Story:

http://www.youtube.com/watch?v=hZtNbUhr6qQ

Ben Comen is a high school student with cerebral palsy whose positive attitude and effort allowed him to participate on his high school cross-country team and beat his personal best time by the time he graduated. This Other-Study video is 8:50 in length.

Focus questions for either the Patrick Willis or Ben Comen Other-Studies may include:

◊ *As you watch the video, identify at least two different circumstances or situations where (Patrick's/Ben's) attitude and/or effort contributed to a positive outcome. Provide the details regarding what led you to this conclusion.*

◊ *What stands out about (Patrick's/Ben's) approach to a positive attitude and best effort?*

C. Michael Jordan - Maybe It's My Fault:

http://www.youtube.com/watch?v=_-EyRUgp9Mk

This Other-Study video is a commercial featuring Michael Jordan and the attitude and effort required to achieve his professional basketball goals. This Other-Study video is 1:02 minutes in length.

Focus questions for the Michael Jordan Other-Study may include:

◊ *As you watch the video, identify how Michael Jordan's message applies to being successful in achieving one's goals.*

◊ *What stands out about Michael Jordan's approach to a positive attitude and best effort?*

6. Wrap up the Other-Study activity by facilitating a brainstorm of favorite examples of when attitude and effort led to improvement. Record the brainstorm examples either on the board or chart paper.

7. Explain the notion of **drivers** and **preventers** of a positive attitude and strong effort. Use the templates in #2 in the Student Workbook for the activity to follow. Introduction to this activity may sound something like this:

◊   *In spite of many real world examples, it still can be challenging to put this formula into practice in our own lives — especially when we apply it to things we don't particularly like or aren't particularly good at.*

◊   *It's helpful to think about factors that drive or encourage positive attitude and effort, and factors that detract from positive attitude and effort.*

◊   *For example, when you like something you will most likely have a positive attitude and good effort. On the other hand, when you don't like to do something, the chances of having a negative, or indifferent attitude, and minimal or poor effort are greater.*

◊   *When faced with a challenge, you can choose to complain, make excuses, be defensive, defeated, or resistant to change, get angry and frustrated, give up too soon, quit or cheat.*

◊   *There are strategies you can use to overcome a negative attitude or lack of effort. For example, you can choose to be open to new challenges instead of making excuses.*

◊   *In small groups, work on identifying some typical **drivers** and **preventers** and identifying strategies to positively influence each factor (#2 in the Student Workbook).*

◊   *As a group, complete Step 1 on the two templates (remember to brainstorm both drivers and preventers).*

◊   *Once your group has finished your brainstorm, swap with another group. Review what the group wrote and add to their brainstorm.*

◊   *Once the brainstorm is complete, move forward with Steps 2 and 3 on the templates.*

◊   *Be prepared to share the most important factors and the reasoning your group used to identify the contributing/detracting factors and strategies for improvement.*

8.   Facilitate a discussion and allow groups to share their drivers/preventers results.

Factors that encourage or drive attitude and effort include: when you're naturally good at something, when you can understand the purpose and importance of the goal/activity, and when you can see its short- and long-term benefit(s). Factors that can prevent or get in the way of attitude and effort are things like not being naturally good at something, not seeing the purpose of the goal/activity or its short- or long-term benefit(s), lacking confidence in yourself, or other simple things like being hungry, tired, sad, or mad.

Strategies to positively influence drivers and preventers of attitude and effort may include: be open to new challenges; be hopeful, confident, and enthusiastic; keep trying and continue persevering; learn from your mistakes and seek outside help.

Closure & Assessment:

9. Have students conduct a Self-Study and plot their attitude and effort toward:

   A = Attitude and Effort toward school/education

   B = Attitude and Effort toward work (current or most recent employment)

   C = Attitude and Effort toward relationships with friends and family.

10. Finally, close the lesson with a summary of what they learned and what their future steps might be.

Extension:

11. **Other-Study:** Choose from the Other-Study videos below, or use one of your own. As students watch the video, have them record specific evidence of positive attitude and effort. Facilitate a discussion to debrief their findings.

    Brandon's story - long

    http://www.youtube.com/watch?v=kLpUZ4W4ECI

    Division I Wrestler

    http://www.youtube.com/watch?v=NikVGvYIocs

Pursuit of Happyness - Protect your dreams

http://www.youtube.com/watch?v=MEGSiX0JA-s

12. **Self-Study:** Have students identify a specific goal they wish to achieve in the next two to three weeks. Encourage students to choose a goal that provides them with a challenge. Have them use the AEI Rubric to self-assess the current state of their attitude and effort, and then identify strategies to either maintain a positive attitude and effort, or to improve their attitude and effort.

13. **Performance/Simulation:** Have students keep a log or journal, as they work through the identified goal. When did things get difficult? Where were you on the AEI rubric? How did you push through? Have students share their goal, strategies and excerpts from their log or journal. Integrate support and challenge into the presentations to allow students to learn from each other and gain support from one another.

14. **Support & Challenge:** Build in opportunities for students to identify and receive the support and challenge necessary to not only reach their goal, but to improve their attitude and effort based on the AEI rubric.

Planning and Reflection

2. Communicating Effectively with Others

Module 2-1: Two-Way Communication

Competency: Use effective communication strategies in diverse contexts and settings

Tools: *Two-Way Communication Basics, Verify and Clarify Strategies, Use Catchable "I"-Statements, Avoid Dart-Style "You"-Statements*

EXCELLENCE with INTEGRITY

TWO-WAY COMMUNICATION BASICS

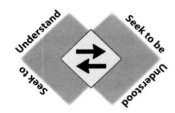

» through active listening that verifies shared understanding and clarifies what is unclear

» by expressing thoughts, feelings and expectations without blame, insult or personal attack

© 2016 Institute for Excellence & Ethics (IEE)   www.excellenceandethics.org

---

EXCELLENCE with INTEGRITY

TWO-WAY COMMUNICATION VERIFY AND CLARIFY STRATEGIES

» Restating to **verify** sounds like:

" *From your point of view, you believe ...* "

" *So, you feel ...* "

" *What I hear you saying is ...* "

» Restating to **clarify** sounds like:

" *Are you saying ... ?* "

" *Is this what you mean ... ?* "

" *Can you explain ... ?* "

© 2016 Institute for Excellence & Ethics (IEE)   www.excellenceandethics.org

---

EXCELLENCE with INTEGRITY

TWO-WAY COMMUNICATION CATCHABLE "I"-STATEMENTS

USE *statements that:*

» honestly and respectfully express your thoughts and feelings;

» focus on finding solutions;

» clarify the goal or expectation;

» sound like:

" *I think ... because ...* "

" *I feel ... because ...* "

" *I plan to ... because ...* "

© 2016 Institute for Excellence & Ethics (IEE)   www.excellenceandethics.org

---

EXCELLENCE with INTEGRITY

TWO-WAY COMMUNICATION DART-STYLE "YOU"-STATEMENTS

AVOID *statements that:*

» divide, distract, and disrespect;

» blame, insult, and attack the personality or character of the other person;

» sound like:

" *You caused this to happen.* "

" *You never do your part.* "

" *You are so stupid.* "

© 2016 Institute for Excellence & Ethics (IEE)   www.excellenceandethics.org

---

Objective

Students will use the Two-Way Communication Basics, Verify and Clarify Strategies, Use Catchable "I"-Statements, Avoid Dart-Style "You"-Statements to improve communication, social skills, and interactions with others.

Overview

1. Students will conduct an Other-Study of a video from the reality TV show, The Colony, in order to identify the factors that prevent effective communication.

2. Students will assess their own communication tendencies through a Self-Study.

3. Students will role-play given scenarios and evaluate the role-plays of their peers to determine the one with the most effective use of Two-Way Communication.

Preparation

1. Determine how you will establish the behavioral norms needed to ensure a positive and productive learning experience for all students.

2. Prepare role-play cards.

3. Determine scoring process for "Class Finals".

4. Prepare external streaming video content:

   a. Review IEE policy regarding use of external content.

   b. "The Colony"

   http://www.discovery.com/tv-shows/other-shows/videos/the-colony-when-gas-runs-out.htm.

Materials

- Role-play scenario cards (sets A, B, C, D).

Module Delivery Steps

Introduction:

1. Have students discuss with a partner (or in small groups) the following quote from Mark Twain to explain what they think the quote means and providing supporting examples from their own personal experiences:

    "The difference between the right word and the almost right word is the difference between the lightning and the lightning bug."

2. Introduce the Two-Way Communication Basics. Introduction of the tool might go something like this:

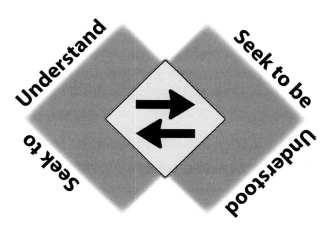

⊘ EXCELLENCE WITH INTEGRITY

TWO-WAY COMMUNICATION BASICS

Seek to Understand
»   through active listening that verifies shared understanding and clarifies what is unclear

Seek to be Understood
»   by expressing thoughts, feelings and expectations without blame, insult or personal attack

© 2016 Institute for Excellence & Ethics (IEE)   www.excellenceandethics.org

◊   *Communication is a foundational skill required for success in school, work, and beyond. Two-Way Communication has a twofold goal of seeking to understand and seeking to be understood.*

◊   *We seek to understand through active listening that verifies shared understanding and clarifies what is unclear. We seek to be understood by using "I"-statements (such as "I think…"; "I feel…"), as opposed to "You"-statements (such as, "you always…"; "you never…"), in order to accurately express our thoughts, feelings and expectations without blame, insult or personal attack.*

3.   Introduce the three 'drill-down' tools: the Verify & Clarify Strategies, Use Catchable "I"-Statements, Avoid Dart-Style "You"-Statements.

4.   Have students take the Two-Way Communication Self-Study, #1 in the Student Workbook.

⊘ EXCELLENCE WITH INTEGRITY

TWO-WAY COMMUNICATION
VERIFY AND CLARIFY STRATEGIES

» **Restating to verify sounds like:**

" *From your point of view, you believe …* "

" *So, you feel …* "

" *What I hear you saying is …* "

» **Restating to clarify sounds like:**

" *Are you saying … ?* "

" *Is this what you mean … ?* "

" *Can you explain … ?* "

TWO-WAY COMMUNICATION
DART-STYLE "YOU"-STATEMENTS

AVOID statements that:

» divide, distract, and disrespect;

» blame, insult, and attack the personality or character of the other person;

» sound like:

" *You caused this to happen.* "

" *You never do your part.* "

" *You are so stupid.* "

TWO-WAY COMMUNICATION
CATCHABLE "I"-STATEMENTS

USE statements that:

» honestly and respectfully express your thoughts and feelings;

» focus on finding solutions;

» clarify the goal or expectation;

» sound like:

" *I think … because …* "

" *I feel … because …* "

" *I plan to … because …* "

    www.excellenceandethics.org

5. After completion of the Self-Study, speaking in general terms, ask students what they noticed about themselves when reflecting on their ability to demonstrate Two-Way Communication skills.

6. Conduct the Two-Way Communication Other-Study. Introduce the following clip from the reality TV show, The Colony, which puts together people with different skills, abilities and expertise (some have advanced degrees, some have applied experiences) into a survival situation where they must work together to survive using only the materials they have in this old factory and their shared knowledge and skills. Have students identify what they believe is preventing the group from communicating effectively.

    "The Colony"

http://www.discovery.com/tv-shows/other-shows/videos/the-colony-when-gas-runs-out.htm

7. Facilitate a group discussion about what's getting in the way of effective communication (ask for specific examples wherever possible).

    Possible answers include:

    » *They don't listen to each other, they don't ask clarifying questions, they don't verify that they understand each other's thinking, and they attack each other instead of the problem at hand, they don't respect each other's abilities.*

8. Continue the discussion by focusing on the use of questions to verify and clarify seeking examples from the group where the individuals in the video might have made better use of verify clarify questions, which might sound like:

    ◊ *When we use restatement to clarify and verify our understanding it:*

      » *Validates a person's thoughts and feelings.*

      » *Corrects misunderstandings, false assumptions, and misinterpretations.*

      » *It does not deny a person's perceptions, dispute a person's feelings, ignore a person's opinions, refute a person's experiences, or degrade a person's character.*

    ◊ *And include examples like the following:*

Mike could have helped to clarify and verify his understanding of the group's plan:

> » *What I hear you saying is that the vent you built is where the dangerous gas will be released?*
>
> » *So you feel that it's not going to backfire and blow up?*
>
> » *Can you explain to me how the gas gets released?*

Vlad, John, and Morgan could have clarified and verified their understanding of Mike's concerns:

> » *So you think the gas will build up and explode?*
>
> » *Are you saying we should scrap the whole thing, or just improve one part of it?*
>
> » *Can you explain how we could prevent it from blowing up?*

9. Now focus the discussion on the effective use of "I"-Statements (and the downside of "You"-Statements) drawing out examples from the video, which might sound like:

> ◊ *In this video emotions are running high. They're communicating at each other, not with each other. The exchange reveals a form of dart-style "You"-statements, which divide, distract and disrespect.*
>
> ◊ *These "You"-statements are like darts; they blame, insult, and/or attack the personality and character of the other person. They often make the problem worse because they lead to hard feelings. Also, when you throw darts at somebody, they're likely to throw darts back at you.*
>
> ◊ *But, if you want to communicate so that you are understood, avoid dart-style "You"-statements and instead use catchable "I"-statements.*
>
> ◊ *Effective "I"-statements express thoughts and feelings and clarify the goal or expectation. They are respectful, solution-centered, and contribute to effective and efficient problem solving.*
>
> ◊ *"I"-statement examples are simple statements of what I think, feel, or intend to do with a straightforward explanation of why.*
>
> ◊ *In the Colony this might have sounded like "Hey Morgan, I feel angry that you told me to get out. I don't think my experience is valued. I am going back inside to try a different approach." "Hey Mike, I feel resentful and frustrated when you yell at me. I think that our plan is solid. I would like to try it and if doesn't work we'll seek your advice."*

◊ *These "I"-statements express thoughts and feelings and clarify the goal or expectation. They are respectful, solution-centered, and contribute to effective and efficient problem solving. "I"-statements don't mean that we have no creative conflicts, that we all agree with each other. However, they do help our thoughts and feelings and actions be more accurately understood by others; and, they prevent hard feelings that can really make working together difficult.*

Guided Practice:

10. Divide the group into four groups. Ensure the room is arranged so the students can move and conduct the role-plays.

11. Provide each group with a set of Role-Play Scenario Cards. The teams select which role-play scenario they want to begin with (Scenario A, B, C or D). After the group has chosen a scenario, determine which two students will participate in the first role-play (there will be 3 more opportunities). The students choose roles at random. The students should not share the information on their role-play card with other members of the group.

12. Have each group select a timekeeper from the members not participating in the role-play.

13. Explain that the two chosen students from each group will role-play their chosen scenario for no longer than 1 minute 30 seconds, while the other members of the team score the role-play using the Two-Way Communication role-play score card (#3 in the Student Workbook). The goal for the students in the role-play is to obtain the highest score by demonstrating the skills in the Two-Way Communication.

14. Prior to the start of the role-play, review the score card in #2 in the Student Workbook, so all are familiar with the scoring system and refer to the brainstorming session to remind students of the types of phrases and words they should be listening for.

15. When all groups have had the opportunity to work through all four sets of role-plays, determine which role-play scenario in each group scored the highest. These groups will have the opportunity to move to the finals.

Closure & Assessment:

16. Facilitate the finals by having the pair with the highest score from each group do their role-play for everyone. Encourage students to attempt to increase their score in the finals by using the Two-Way Communication more effectively.

Determine how to facilitate the scoring process to reach consensus on which group scored the most points.

17. Close the lesson by asking students to review the Self-Study they completed earlier (#1 in the Student Workbook). Facilitate a discussion asking students to reflect on whether the tendencies they identified in the Self-Study played out to be true in the role-play scenarios. Possible prompts may include:

◊ *Were you effective in the role-play at the Two-Way Communication skills you had identified as being effective at? Why? Why not?*

◊ *Were the Two-Way Communication skills you identified as challenging, actually difficult for you to use in the role-play? Why? Why not?*

◊ *What makes using these skills easy or difficult?*

18. Close the lesson by reiterating the value of the Two-Way Communication. Share with students that according to a Harris Interactive/Wall Street Journal Business School Survey (2007), "***Communication and interpersonal skills remain at the top of the list of what matters most to [job] recruiters.***"

Extension:

19. **Other-Study:** Reality television may be a pop-culture phenomenon, but it is also a great genre to look to for Other-Studies on communication. Using clips from shows like Amazing Race, Survivor, Dinner Impossible, etc., have students analyze the level of seeking to understand and to be understood present in the students' communication by using the "I"-Statements/"You"-Statements Tools.

20. **Self-Study:** Ask students to track their communications for a given period (for example: three days) and use the Two-Way Communication

Rubric to reflect on and analyze their comfort level and effectiveness of the Two-Way Communication.

21. **Performance/Simulation:** Have groups of students (or individuals) write their own communication scenario cards. Paper-clip the scenario card sets together, then put all sets into a hat or box. Have two students come to the front of the room, draw a set of scenario cards, and engage in a scenario role-play. At the conclusion of each role-play, allow participating students first to self-assess their own communication using the Two-Way Communication Tools, then have their peers in the audience share their assessment also using the tools.

22. **Support & Challenge:** For high school students: Host a community parent night to teach the Two-Way Communication Tools to parents and guardians. Provide parents/guardians with insights into what common struggles students demonstrate and suggest effective approaches for parents/guardians to help their child further develop their ability to communicate effectively by using the Two-Way Communication Tools. Consider having the students role-play at the event and develop opportunities for parents/guardians to role-play with their child.

Planning and Reflection

Role-Play Scenario Cards

Scenario A Role: Student	Scenario A Role: Teacher/Professor
Scenario: Your teacher has assigned a group project that requires a great deal of work to be done outside of class. In order to make the due date, the majority of the work will need to be done during break week. You, and most of your group members, were planning to be away. **Initiate a conversation with your teacher/professor to discuss changing the project due date.**	**Scenario:** You have assigned a group project to your class which requires a significant amount of work to be done outside of class. In order to make the due date, the majority of the work will need to be done during break week. You were aware of the break week when you assigned the project, but went ahead and assigned the project anyway believing the students should be able to manage. **One of your students wants to have a conversation with you to discuss changing the project due date.**
Scenario B Role: College-Bound Sibling	**Scenario B Role: Younger (High School-Aged) Sibling**
Scenario: You are leaving for college, leaving a younger high school-aged sibling behind at home. You want to take one of the two gaming systems, which belong to the entire family, to college with you. You didn't really discuss this with anyone; you just put the system of your choice in with the other supplies you are taking to college. Your younger sibling is very upset and has complained to your parents. **You need to have a conversation with your sibling to try to work out the situation.**	**Scenario:** Your older sibling is leaving for college and wants to take one of the two gaming systems, which belong to the entire family, to college with him/her. He/she didn't discuss this with anyone in the family; he/she just put the system of his/her choice in with the other supplies he/she is taking to college. You are very upset and complained to your parents. **Your parents have let your brother/sister know he/she needs to have a conversation with you to work out the situation.**
Scenario C Role: Parent	**Scenario C Role: Teenager**
Scenario: You have always required your teenager to provide you with access to their Facebook page, so you can monitor what is posted. Generally, this is no big deal, but recently you have actually posted your teen's status and also chatted with available friends. You do not see a problem with this behavior, but your teen is very upset. **Your teenager wants to have a conversation with you about posting and chatting while logged in on their Facebook account.**	**Scenario:** Your parent requires access to your Facebook page in order to monitor what is being posted. Generally, this is not a big deal, but recently your parent has posted your status and also chatted with available friends. You are very upset about this, but know if you just change your log-in, your parent will cut you off completely from the internet. **You need to have a conversation with your parent about posting and chatting while logged in on your Facebook account.**
Scenario D Role: Employee	**Scenario D Role: Employer**
Scenario: Your boss originally hired you to work 8-12 hours a week in the evenings and on weekends. When you were hired, the boss knew you were in sports and agreed you could provide a monthly schedule of your availability and he'd work with your schedule. Recently, the boss has begun scheduling you for more than 12 hours a week and during the times you indicated you were unavailable to work. **You really need this job, so you can't just quit; therefore, you need to have a conversation with your boss about the situation.**	**Scenario:** You hired a high-school student to work 8-12 hours a week in the evenings and on weekends. When you hired the student, you were aware the student was involved in sports and you agreed he/she could provide you with a monthly schedule of his/her availability and you'd work with their schedule. You recently had an employee quit, so you've been scheduling the student more than 12 hours a week and during times when he/she indicated they were not available. **The student employee does not want to quit, but needs to have a conversation with you about the situation.**

Planning and Reflection

Module 2-2: Preparing to Communicate

Competency: Use social awareness & interpersonal skills to establish & maintain positive relationships

Tool: *Prepare to Communicate Checklist*

EXCELLENCE with INTEGRITY

PREPARE TO COMMUNICATE CHECKLIST

1. Know **who** you are communicating with and **how** best to respect and connect with them.

   who?   *how?*

2. Determine **what** outcomes you want to achieve—and avoid.

   what?

3. Consider **when** and **where** will be the most favorable context for the communication.

   when?   *where?*

© 2016 Institute for Excellence & Ethics (IEE)   www.excellenceandethics.org

Objective

Students will use the Prepare to Communicate Checklist to improve social awareness and interpersonal skills to establish and maintain positive relationships.

Overview

1. Students will analyze and critique the communication skills as presented in two scenes from Remember the Titans using the Prepare to Communicate Checklist.

2. Working in partnerships, students will choose a real-life scenario to create their own communication plan.

Preparation

1. Determine how you will establish the behavioral norms needed to ensure a positive and productive learning experience for all students.

2. Prepare external streaming video content:

   a. Review IEE policy regarding use of external content.

   b. "Remember the Titans, #1"

   https://www.youtube.com/watch?v=dUTJK0TOmyY

   c. "Remember the Titans, #2"

   https://www.youtube.com/watch?v=lH1SKGXU81U.

Module Delivery Steps

Introduction:

1. Begin the lesson with a discussion of the following quote from John Powell: "*Communication works for those who work at it.*"

   Discussion Prompt:

   ◊ *What kind of work do you need to do in order to communicate well? When was a time you practiced what you wanted to say before you spoke? Why did you rehearse what you wanted to say?*

   (Possible Answers: Wanted to be sure I got what I wanted, to be sure that things didn't go badly, to overcome nerves, to be sure the person I was talking to really understood what I was trying to say, etc.)

2. Have students complete the Self-Study listed in #1 in the Student Work-book.

3. Debrief the Self-Study by asking students to share insights from their self-reflections.

4. Display and introduce the Prepare to Communicate Checklist for use during the remainder of the lesson. Introduction of the tool might go something like this:

   ◊ *Effective communication is a foundational skill required for success in school, work, and beyond. When you take a few simple steps to prepare yourself, you can reduce anxiety and improve the quality of your communication.*

   ◊ *Communication is essential for positive and productive relation-ships, since it allows us to build consensus and resolve conflicts. To increase the chances of positive outcomes and decrease the chances of negative outcomes, preparation is essential prior to communicat-ing.*

   ◊ *The Prepare to Communicate Checklist shows you 3 steps that will help you do that:*

   » *Know who you're communicating with and how best to respect and connect with them.*

» *Determine what outcomes you want to achieve—and avoid.*

» *Consider when and where will be the most favorable context for communication.*

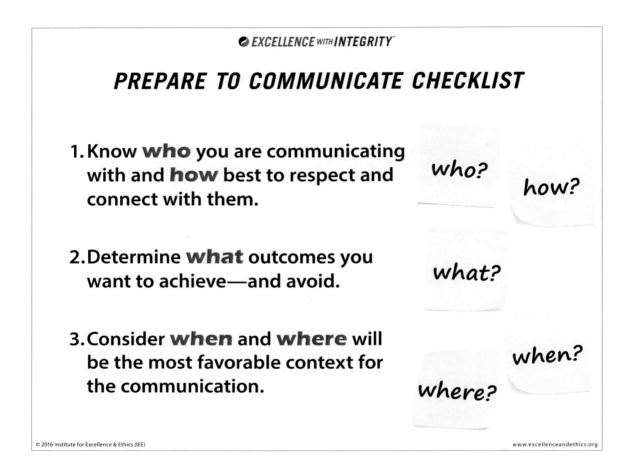

Guided Practice:

5. Introduce the activity by explaining that the activity that follows will make use of two clips from the movie, *Remember the Titans*. The clips will show how poor timing and execution of an initial communication leads to a very bad outcome initially for Gary, but how later Gary skillfully and effectively uses communication skills that earns the respect and trust of his coach. Explanation may sound something like this:

◊ *We're going to observe two clips from the movie, Remember the Titans. This is an inspirational movie that shows the challenges of racial integration in athletics. This is an inspirational sports movie. But at its core it's a movie about human communication. Many of the most dramatic scenes involve white and black characters learning to respect and connect with one another—two hallmarks of effective communication. We'll be using the Prepare to Communicate Checklist to critique the two clips, and as a guide for more effective personal communication.*

6. Introduce the first clip and activity #2 on the Student Materials. The introduction may sound something like this:

◊ *In this first clip we observe football team on its first day as they prepare to leave for training camp. Coach Boone, the new coach played by Denzel Washington, will be responsible for integrating black and white players and coaches. Coach Boone has not yet met Gary. As you watch, see if you can identify evidence that Gary intentionally prepared for the conversation he was about to have. Take a look at #2 on your handout—the three preparation components in column A. As you watch, use column B to cite evidence you see/hear to support what Gary did well (or not well) in his communication with his new coach.*

7. Have students watch video clip #1 from Remember the Titans.

https://www.youtube.com/watch?v=dUTJK0TOmyY

8. Have students complete in small groups #2, Column C on the Student Materials. Your prompt might sound something like this:

◊ *Now that you've watched the clip, how would you have prepared differently for this meeting if you were Gary and wanted to more effectively respect and connect with your new Coach? Jot down some of your ideas in the boxes in Column C.*

9. Facilitate a discussion on the evidence students identified when watching the first clip. Discussion prompts:

◊ *What evidence did you see from the coach's reaction that indicated how effective Gary was in this first exchange with his new coach?*

◊ *What notes did you make of ways you prepared differently to:*

» *Determine the outcomes you want to achieve and avoid.*

» *Know who you're communicating with and how best to respect and connect with them.*

»   *Consider where and when will be the most favorable context for the conversation.*

◊   *It's important to remember that in this clip Gary got things off on very bad note with his new Coach. And, one might understand why Coach Boone responded as he did to make it clear to everyone—players, coaches, and parents—who was in charge of this team. However, one could also argue that Coach Boone could have responded differently. What specifically might Coach Boone have done differently?*

◊   *You may not be in a similar situation as a team captain meeting a new coach. But the point is that it's essential to prepare to effectively communicate for the situations when the result of the communication is important to you. For example, what if you have to meet with your teacher after school—does it make a difference where you sit? What if you pulled a chair up to the teacher's desk instead of sitting in your seat or standing over him/her while they are sitting? Instead of saying "you gave me a bad grade," what if you asked, "Is there anything I can do to raise my grade or anything I might do to better prepare in the future?"*

◊   *Even when some preparation has been done, that doesn't always mean that everything will go smoothly. But a little preparation can go a long way to achieving the outcomes you want—and avoiding the really bad outcomes you don't want to see happen.*

◊   *Little things make a big difference when it comes to communication and that's why it's critical to prepare to communicate.*

10. Introduce the second *Remember the Titans* video clip and activity #3 on the Student Materials. The introduction to the activity may sound something like this:

◊   *In the first video clip we observed that Gary's first interaction with Coach Boone went very poorly. In the second video clip we're about to watch, later in the movie, we observe a very different kind of communication between Gary and Coach Boone. As you watch this clip see if you can identify evidence that Gary has intentionally prepared for the conversation with his Coach. If you find evidence of preparation, place a check in the box in Column B and make a quick note explaining what you observed.*

11. Have students watch the second Remember the Titans video clip.

https://www.youtube.com/watch?v=lH1SKGXU81U

12. Have students complete #3 Column C on the Student Materials. Your prompt may sound something like this:

    ◊ *We see a very different kind of exchange between Gary and his Coach in this second clip. In Column C, jot down some observations regarding why you think Gary's communication strategies (Column A and B) worked so well. Why is Coach more open to Gary's message because of the specific things that Gary does well in this communication?*

13. Facilitate a discussion with students comparing and contrasting the two exchanges between Gary and Coach Boone and the difference in the kinds of respect and connection that the two have earned. (It may also be helpful to make note of the respect and maturity Gary shows in his final communication with his teammate Ray. Ray is not happy, but the communication is still civil and Gary has clearly chosen the right time, place, and strategy for delivering this difficult message).

14. Transition to the next activity, which might sound something like this:

    ◊ *Okay, so we may not be captains on sports team during a difficult time of racial integration, but studying these examples allowed us to better understand the importance of preparing to communicate and the components of strong communication skills. Think about where you are now in terms of preparing to communicate. Go back to the rubric on your Student Materials that we've been using, what do you consistently do? What can you do better? In this class, how can we support each other to be strong communicators?*

    ◊ *Let's look at the scenarios in #4 on the Student Materials, which hopefully provide some examples that are more relevant to our own daily lives.*

    ◊ *What are other types of scenarios you encounter where preparing to communicate would be beneficial?*

15. In partnerships, have students choose a scenario (either one provided in #4 in the Student Workbook, or have students brainstorm additional scenarios, or provide others yourself) and begin to develop a communication plan by answering the questions listed in #5 in the Student Workbook.

16. When students have discussed the questions, have them write their plan to respect and connect with others, determine outcomes, and understand the context by using the table in #6 in the Student Workbook.

Once their plan is complete, have partnerships role-play the plan they developed.

Closure & Assessment:

17. Close the lesson by debriefing the activities in #4-6 in the Student Workbook and reiterating the value of the Prepare to Communicate Checklist. Closing comments might begin like this:

    ◊ *Knee-jerk reactions rarely result in effective communication and in most cases cause more harm than good.*

    ◊ *Try using this tool on a daily basis, so the process of thinking before you speak becomes a habit.*

18. Have students reflect in writing on the new knowledge shared today regarding the importance of preparing to communicate by completing #7 in the Student Workbook.

Extension:

19. **Other-Study:** Look for communication scenarios in video clips, movies, literature, etc. and have students analyze the communication exchange using the Prepare to Communicate Checklist. For counter examples, allow students the opportunity to "re-write" the scenario.

20. **Self-Study:** Have students think of a particular communication they need to have and using the rubric on the Student Workbook allow them to plan for and reflect upon the experience.

21. **Performance/Simulation:** Continue to provide a variety of role-plays using topics that resonate with the students (e.g., you want a raise from your boss, you disagree with the dean of students regarding a punishment you've received, you want to ask your parents for permission to do something important to you, etc.). As students use the Prepare to Communicate Checklist, have them explain why they think what they've decided to do will work in the particular situation.

22. **Support & Challenge:** Have each student prepare a communication plan for a particular communication exchange they will soon have. Then have students share their plan with their partners from today's lesson, with each partner giving and receiving feedback. Have students meet again after the communication exchange takes place to discuss how it went and how they can continue to strengthen their preparation for communication.

Planning and Reflection

Module 2-3: Win-Win Negotiation

Competency: Exercise flexibility and willingness to make necessary compromises to accomplish a common goal

Tools: *Win-Win Negotiation Guide and Principled Negotiation Tactics*

Objective

Students will use the Win-Win Negotiation Guide and Principled Negotiation Tactics to learn how to exercise flexibility and willingness to make necessary compromises to accomplish a common goal.

Overview

1. Students will see video examples of different negotiation approaches.
2. Students will learn to identify the elements of Win-Win Negotiation and Principled Negotiation Tactics.

Preparation

1. Determine how you will establish the behavioral norms needed to ensure a positive and productive learning experience for all students.
2. Determine the amount of time allotted for students to plan for their negotiation role play.
3. Determine the amount of time each group will receive to perform their negotiation role play.
4. Prepare external streaming video content:
   a. Review IEE policy regarding use of external content.
   b. "Art of Negotiation"

   http://www.youtube.com/watch?v=ml5A4wlipVg.
   c. "How to Negotiate a Later Curfew"

   http://www.youtube.com/watch?v=kMMwxz2pKu0.

Module Delivery Steps

Introduction:

1. Begin by showing the "Art of Negotiation" YouTube clip. This humorous clip is actually drawing upon some common perceptions we have about negotiation.

   http://www.youtube.com/watch?v=ml5A4wlipVg

2. Have students complete the Self-Study in #1 in the Student Workbook based on the video clip they watched.

3. Facilitate a discussion with students on their current understanding of the term "negotiation."

   Discussion Prompts:

   ◊ *What do you think of when you hear the word "negotiation"?*

   ◊ *What does it mean to negotiate successfully?*

   ◊ *Where and when might you utilize negotiation skills in your own life?*

4. Explain to students that today they will be learning a style of Win-Win Negotiation that they will immediately be able to start practicing in school, at work, and in other areas of their lives.

Guided Practice:

5. Introduce the Win-Win Negotiation Guide. Introduction may sound something like this:

   ◊ *Negotiation is essentially finding a balance between the competing needs or ideas of individuals. Negotiation is basically an "I want, You want, We could" process.*

   ◊ *Negotiation is a form of cooperation, a give and take that is needed for successfully working with others. When you are looking to successfully negotiate with others, it is important to remember 3 main steps:*

6. Introduce the second YouTube clip, "How to Negotiate a Later Curfew."

Introduction to the clip may sound something like this:

◊ *When we think of negotiating with others, it is often associated in our mind with emotions like anger, fear, tension, and frustration; and with behaviors like intimidation, argument, trickery, manipulation, and deception. In actuality, successful negotiation is the exact opposite. It is the process by which you compromise in order to make it a win-win situation for all parties involved. In the clip you are about to see, the boy is looking to extend his curfew. When you watch this model of negotiation look for answers to questions in #2 in the Student Workbook.*

"How to Negotiate a Later Curfew" YouTube clip:

http://www.youtube.com/watch?v=kMMwxz2pKu0

7. Facilitate a discussion based on what the students saw in the clip. Discussion points may sound something like this:

    ◊ *You may have noticed that the boy begins the conversation by presenting what he wants and why he wants it. At the beginning of the conversation the boy clearly and thoroughly lays out his needs to his parents using specific talking points.*

    ◊ *These points include evidence to support his argument accompanied by specific examples of where he has successfully handled increased responsibilities in the past.*

    ◊ *There is also evidence that the boy is actively listening to his parents, as they discuss their wants. He listens without arguing or getting upset and he takes notes during the discussion in order to help process the information he is hearing.*

    ◊ *Finally, the boy comes to the negotiation conversation equipped with counter offers, such as an extended curfew trial period, and a willingness to work with his parents to come up with other creative solutions.*

    ◊ *It is through the use of this three-step process—"I want/You want/ We could"—that successful negotiations take place. Keep the model of negotiation you just viewed in mind, as you work with your groups today.*

8. Have students get into small groups for the remainder of the lesson. (Use whatever strategy mixes the students into small groups of 4-6 students. This can be done using a random count off, pre-assigned groups, etc.).

9. Have students read the "Homecoming Canceled" article (provided in the Student Workbook), either silently or with their group.

10. After students have read the article, explain that they will be doing a role-playing activity in which they will negotiate with administrators to reinstate the 1) Car Wreck, 2) Dodge Ball Tournament and 3) Homecoming Dance that were canceled as a result of poor behavior by a few fellow students. Each group's role-playing experience will be conducted in front of entire class. The students that are observing the role-play will be using a rubric (#5 in the Student Workbook) to score the group's overall ability to successfully negotiate a win-win experience.

11. Assign roles or allow students time to decide upon the roles within the group. Suggested roles are: 1-2 administrator(s) and 3-4 students.

12. Give students a specified amount of time to prepare for their negotiation experience. Groups should split up so that "students" and "administrators" can plan for their negotiation experience separately. Explanation may sound something like this:

   ◊ *In order to help you prepare to negotiate, utilize the Principled Negotiation Tactics:*

      » *Know your non-negotiables (ethical and practical).*

      » *Give a little to get a little.*

      » *Seek the maximum good for the maximum number.*

⬤ EXCELLENCE WITH INTEGRITY

PRINCIPLED NEGOTIATION TACTICS

1. Know your practical and ethical non-negotiables.

2. Give a little to get a little.

3. Seek the maximum good for the maximum number.

© 2016 Institute for Excellence & Ethics (IEE)   www.excellenceandethics.org

   ◊ *Remember, as you negotiate, it is important to think about both short- and long-term solutions to this problem; make sure that you are not coming up with a compromise that can make things worse in the long run.*

   ◊ *Use #3 and #4 in your Student Workbook to help you develop your plan for a successful negotiation experience.*

13. Allow groups a specified amount of time to take turns presenting their negotiation role-plays to the class. Using the rubric, have remaining students assess the success of the negotiation experience.

Closure & Assessment:

14. Close the lesson by reiterating and discussing the value of the Win-Win Negotiation Guide and its usefulness for finding balance between the competing needs or ideas of individuals. Closing comments might begin like this:

    ◊ *Negotiation is the process by which you compromise in order to make it a win-win situation for all parties involved. It requires you to clearly and thoroughly articulate your thoughts and ideas, listen to understand the thoughts and ideas of others, and work together to creatively come up with win-win solutions to difficult situations.*

    ◊ *Although negotiation is a skill that can be frequently utilized, there are certain things that you don't negotiate. Any unethical situation or anything that violates your conscience (cheating, lying, stealing, etc.) should not be negotiated. It is important, especially under these circumstances, to know your non-negotiables. know where you won't go and what you won't do.*

    ◊ *Whether it is in group work, or in any kind of relationship, it is especially important to know and respect your own morals, as well as the morals of those you are negotiating with.*

15. Facilitate a closing discussion for the lesson.

    Discussion prompts:

    ◊ *Before today, how would you have defined negotiation?*

    ◊ *How would you define negotiation now?*

    ◊ *What went well during the negotiation role-play activity?*

    ◊ *What part(s) of negotiation do you think you most need work on?*

    ◊ *How specifically can the Win-Win Negotiation Guide help you consider the perspective of others and develop positive and productive relationships?*

Extension:

16. **Other-Study:** Look for examples of negotiation in the news, movies, television shows, and everyday occurrences that students can relate to and have students use a rubric similar to the one used in this lesson to analyze the scenarios.

17. **Self-Study:** Provide students with the opportunity to chart, or track, evidence that supports a negotiation they wish to engage in. Some examples may include evidence of academic responsibility to support a negotiation with the counselor or faculty member to add a class, or advance to a higher level course, etc.

18. **Performance/Simulation:** Use the Win-Win Negotiation Guide as a means to facilitate constructive critique. Provide scenarios, or allow students to share their negotiation process and provide opportunity for constructive critique.

19. **Support & Challenge:** Enlist the support of the guidance counselor and/or social worker to address the importance of identifying and expressing ethical non-negotiables in social settings. Have students identify the negotiation strategies teens use to melt the resistance of others. Common social scenarios that students often identify as peer pressure may include drinking alcohol, trying drugs, engaging in sexual activity, participating in illegal behavior such as stealing, trespassing, vandalism, etc.

Planning and Reflection

Planning and Reflection

3. Developing the Habits for Excellence

Module 3-1: The Habits for Excellence

Competency: Set internal standards for excellence

Tools: *Habits for Excellence and Habits for Excellence Personal Profile*

⊘ EXCELLENCE WITH INTEGRITY

HABITS FOR EXCELLENCE

1. Practice with **focus, intensity, consistency,** and **persistence.**

2. Find the **will to start** and **the grit** to stick with it.

3. Seek **capable coaching** and **constructive critique.**

© 2016 Institute for Excellence & Ethics (IEE)   www.excellenceandethics.org

---

⊘ EXCELLENCE WITH INTEGRITY

HABITS FOR EXCELLENCE PERSONAL PROFILE

Please indicate how closely the statements below reflect your own attitudes and beliefs.	Not true for me	Sort of true for me	Definitely true for me
1. I believe that through hard work I can improve at most anything.			
2. I believe that natural ability is the most important factor in determining success.			
3. I worry about how my abilities compare to those of others.			
4. I am afraid of failure.			
5. I am always looking for ways to improve.			
6. I often struggle to motivate myself to work harder.			
7. I look for challenges and opportunities that test and stretch my abilities.			
8. I often settle for "good enough."			
9. I believe you've either got ability or you don't, and that no amount of practice can change that.			
10. I am able to make myself practice to improve skills that I am not good at.			
11. I am able to take constructive criticism and advice and use it to improve.			
12. I am able to work hard on my own to improve my skills and abilities.			
13. I am able to engage in intense and concentrated practice for extended periods of time.			
14. I am able to practice a skill over and over until I have it mastered.			
15. I am able to make myself practice to improve at things I don't like.			

© 2016 Institute for Excellence & Ethics (IEE)   www.excellenceandethics.org

---

Objective

Students will use the Habits for Excellence and Habits for Excellence Personal Profile to develop their understanding of the essential strategies for developing their talents and abilities.

Overview

1. Students will conduct a Self-Study using the Habits for Excellence Personal Profile.

2. Students will participate in a discussion focused on an Other-Study on the children's book author Jarrett J. Krosoczka.

3. Students will demonstrate understanding of the Habits for Excellence by creating children's books that explain what the Habits are and how to get them to "get good" at something.

Preparation

1. Determine how you will establish the behavioral norms needed to ensure a positive and productive learning experience for all students.

2. Determine timing and procedures for children's book creation and book presentations.

3. Prepare external streaming video content:

    a. Review IEE policy regarding use of external content.

    b. "Author/Illustrator Jarrett J. Krosoczka"

    https://www.youtube.com/watch?v=BRMwegVqv6M.

    c. "Author Kathleen Cushman: *What It Takes to 'Get Good': Fires in the Mind*"

    http://edge.ascd.org/video/what-it-takes-to-39-get-good-39-fires-in-the-mind.

    d. "How Bad Do You Want It?"

    https://www.youtube.com/watch?v=lsSC2vx7zFQ

    e. "*Building Habits, Breaking Habits* by Owen Fitzpatrick"

    https://www.youtube.com/watch?v=CojSlsMwDOg

Materials

- Paper for students to create their book.
- Markers/colored pencils for illustrations.

Module Delivery Steps

Introduction:

1.   Introduce the Habits for Excellence Personal Profile.

◉ EXCELLENCE WITH INTEGRITY

HABITS FOR EXCELLENCE PERSONAL PROFILE

Please indicate how closely the statements below reflect your own attitudes and beliefs.	Not true for me	Sort of true for me	Definitely true for me
1. I believe that through hard work I can improve at most anything.			
2. I believe that natural ability is the most important factor in determining success.			
3. I worry about how my abilities compare to those of others.			
4. I am afraid of failure.			
5. I am always looking for ways to improve.			
6. I often struggle to motivate myself to work harder.			
7. I look for challenges and opportunities that test and stretch my abilities.			
8. I often settle for "good enough."			
9. I believe you've either got ability or you don't, and that no amount of practice can change that.			
10. I am able to make myself practice to improve skills that I am not good at.			
11. I am able to take constructive criticism and advice and use it to improve.			
12. I am able to work hard on my own to improve my skills and abilities.			
13. I am able to engage in intense and concentrated practice for extended periods of time.			
14. I am able to practice a skill over and over until I have it mastered.			
15. I am able to make myself practice to improve at things I don't like.			

www.excellenceandethics.org

◊   *The Habits for Excellence Personal Profile provides a Self-Study for you to reflect on your ideas, beliefs and behaviors regarding the development of your talents and abilities. There are no right or wrong answers; this profile is simply meant to assist you in identifying areas of strength to build upon, and areas of growth for improving. So do your best to honestly assess your current beliefs and behaviors.*

◊   *Complete the Habit for Excellence Personal Profile (#1 in the Student Workbook). As you complete the Profile, think about how you are most of the time, not just with things you like or are good at, or just things you don't like or struggle with. We will be discussing these Profiles together as a group, but you will be able to choose what you want to share with your classmates and what you would like to keep to yourself.*

2. Once students have completed their Habits for Excellence Personal Profile, facilitate a group discussion. Introduction to the discussion may start like this:

◊   *Whatever your current Habits for Excellence Profile looks like, it provides you with important self-knowledge about your habits and overall approach for developing your talents and abilities.*

»   *What stands out to you? What obvious areas of strength emerge?*

»   *How about areas for improvement?*

»   *Why is this kind of information important for each of us to have?*

◊   *Additional talking points/prompts for discussion:*

»   *Self-knowledge helps us understand the habits we can turn to when we're struggling to master something (our 'go-to' strengths or habits). This knowledge also helps us to see areas to watch out for when we're struggling to "get good" at something (the habits that get in the way of our growth).*

»   *How could you use the knowledge from your Personal Profile in an interview or a tryout to convince someone that you have the potential to excel?*

»   *Self-knowledge of your own Habits for Excellence is an excellent way to help you stand out from the crowd. The Habits provide you with a way to go beyond performance indicators, like grades, GPA, or test scores; your ability to speak to your practice habits, your drive, and your coachability must also be addressed.*

»   *The Habits for Excellence Personal Profile can provide you with an honest assessment of past struggles, failures, and how you've grown. For example, explaining to an interviewer that you didn't like to practice things that were difficult, or that you struggled to seek outside help would help them understand why your performance may have suffered and how you've learned and grown from that experience.*

»   *The Habits for Excellence Personal Profile can also provide credible evidence of reasons to believe in your potential for future success. Performance measures demonstrate what you've done in the past, but if you also can persuade an interviewer that you're willing to work hard, be coachable, and that you have determination and grit, they're more likely to believe in your future success.*

3.   Introduce the Habits for Excellence.

⊘ *EXCELLENCE WITH INTEGRITY*

HABITS FOR EXCELLENCE

1. **Practice with focus, intensity, consistency, and persistence.**

2. **Find the will to start and the grit to stick with it.**

3. **Seek capable coaching and constructive critique.**

◊ *The Personal Profile is linked directly to the Habits for Excellence Tool, which is rooted in the research on expert performance and talent development, including* Mindset *(Dweck, 2006),* Drive *(Pink, 2009), and work by several other top researchers who study the factors and habits that help individuals get the most from their natural talents and abilities.*

◊ *The Habits for Excellence represent the three essential factors identified in the research. Taken together, these three habits are what will allow you to maximize your potential for excellence in any field or endeavor.*

  » *First, maximizing your potential for excellence requires that you practice with focus, intensity, consistency, and persistence.*

  » *Second, maximizing your potential for excellence requires that you find the will to start and the grit to stick with it.*

  » *Finally, maximizing your potential for excellence requires that you seek capable coaching and constructive critique.*

Guided Practice:

4.   Conduct the following Other-Study:

"Author/Illustrator Jarrett J. Krosoczka"

https://www.youtube.com/watch?v=BRMwegVqv6M

Introduction to the clip may sound like this:

◊   *How hard could it be to get a simple children's book published? In the clip you are about to watch, you will see children's book author, Jarrett J. Krosoczka, discussing the process it took to get his first book published. While we often think great authors, athletes, and musicians are lucky or that success somehow comes easier for them, this video provides some insight into how much time and effort it took Jarrett to achieve his goal of getting a book publishing company to notice his ideas and efforts. As you watch, look for evidence of the Habits for Excellence (#2 in the Student Workbook).*

  »   *Notice where Jarrett practiced with focus, intensity, consistency, and persistence.*

  »   *Watch to see how he found the will to start and the grit to stick with it.*

  »   *Watch to see where he sought capable coaching and constructive critique.*

5.   As a whole class, discuss evidence from the video that Jarrett demonstrated the Habits for Excellence as he worked towards his goal of having one of his books published. Possible discussion points may include:

◊   *Jarrett started practicing with focus, intensity, consistency, and persistence when he was very young. He continued these habits by going to college where he studied drawing and painting. He took many classes where he practiced his skills.*

◊   *Jarrett started his journey toward publication by sending postcards to publishers. Although the first fifty postcards yielded no response, he continued to stick with it by sending out fifty more. Over a two-year period Jarrett revised his postcards and continued to send them out to over a hundred different publishers. As a result of his grit and determination, Random House responded and became interested in his work.*

> ◊ *Jarrett seeks coaching and constructive critique through the writing process and his publisher, Random House. He brainstorms, revises, rewrites, constructs story maps, receives feedback from peers and publishers, and continues to improve his work throughout the process.*

6. Divide the class into pairs for the remainder of the lesson. (Use whatever strategy mixes up the students. This can be done using a random count off, pre-assigned groups, etc.).

7. Explain to students that they will be writing a short book that will teach the Habits for Excellence to elementary-age students. This book will essentially be about showing others how to "get good" at something. Explanation may sound something like this:

> ◊ *As you saw in the video clip, it takes all of the Habits for Excellence working together if you truly want to "get good" at something. Sometimes the best way to understand an idea is try and teach it to somebody else. Today you will be working with your partner to develop, design, and write a short children's book in order to present the Habits for Excellence and explain how they are essential for developing talents and abilities, and how with the Habits for Excellence you can achieve almost anything you set your mind to.*

> ◊ *You may choose any topic to write on, from skateboarding to flying a kite. Your book will describe what it takes to work through the Habits for Excellence when striving to "get good."*

> ◊ *This book can be written in a narrative style with typical story elements, such as characters, plot, setting, problem, and solution, or it can be more of a non-fiction "how-to" style of book.*

*If students need models to view before beginning their children's book, consider having the following for viewing: *Wilma Unlimited*; *Thank You, Mr. Falker*; *The Little Engine that Could*.

> ◊ *Begin by brainstorming some topics to write about with your partner. Use your own experiences to come up with stories of how you developed your talents and abilities, or use other examples that you think provide a powerful story demonstrating the Habits for Excellence (what kind of practice, what kind of willpower and determination, what kind of coaching and constructive criticism did it take). (Step 1 in #3 in the Student Workbook).*

> ◊ *Then develop a plan for what will go on each of the pages in your book. (Step 2 in #3 in the Student Workbook).*

    ◊   *When you've finished the two preliminary planning steps, create your Habits for Excellence children's book! (Step 3 in #3 in the Student Workbook).*

8. Give groups a specified amount of time to prepare their children's book. While they are preparing their pieces, check with each group to ensure that they are making appropriate progress and in order to answer any questions they may have.

9. Allow groups a specified amount of time to take turns presenting their children's books. Utilize the Other-Study from the introduction as a common example when discussing each group's book.

Closure & Assessment:

10. Wrap up the lesson by sharing one or more of the following Other-Studies, which explore what it takes to get really good at something. After viewing, discuss the interesting, useful, and motivational insights gained by students.

"Author Kathleen Cushman: *What It Takes to 'Get Good': Fires in the Mind*"

http://edge.ascd.org/video/what-it-takes-to-39-get-good-39-fires-in-the-mind

"How Bad Do You Want It?"

https://www.youtube.com/watch?v=lsSC2vx7zFQ

"*Building Habits, Breaking Habits* by Owen Fitzpatrick"

https://www.youtube.com/watch?v=CojSlsMwDOg

11. Close the lesson by reviewing the Habits for Excellence and reinforcing the tool's importance. Closing may sound something like this:

    ◊   *While it's convenient to believe that some people are just born successful, that it comes easier for them, that they are just lucky, or that they became successful overnight, scientific research doesn't sup-*

port these beliefs. In reality, *"successful people have formed the habit of doing things that failures don't like to do"* (Albert Gray).

Extension:

12. **Other-Study:** Have students do research on people both in and out of the public eye who put the Habits for Excellence into action in order to make the most of their natural talents and achieve their goals. You can use popular examples; however, it can also be powerful to draw from examples of current or former students, or examples from within your content areas (e.g., writers, scientists, inventors, or entrepreneurs).

13. **Self-Study:** Have students reflect in writing on a talent, skill, or ability that they would like develop (or "get good" at, as is stated in the Cushman video). It can be something they are not naturally good at, and/or something they are naturally good at. Have them create a Habits for Excellence plan for how they can use each of the three habits to make the most of their ability and "get good." During this time, have students return to their Personal Profiles and identify strengths and areas for improvement.

14. **Performance/Simulation:** Have students share their books with elementary-age students. Have students highlight the Habits for Excellence Tool by bringing along copies of the Tool and/or creating an adapted version of the Tool written specifically for the age level they will present their books to.

15. **Support & Challenge:** Make a laminated copy of the Habits for Excellence Personal Profile for each student. Once per week, have each student fill out a Personal Profile based on how they are feeling after completing most of the week. As the weeks continue, have students make observations on how their Personal Profile changes and/or stays the same, and make commitments to strategies they can use to improve their use of the Habits for Excellence (e.g., have students write one strategy on a 3x5 index card and call it a "commitment card," then have them tape the card to the bottom of their profile). Allow students to regularly discuss this monitoring practice and what they are learning from it.

Planning and Reflection

Module 3-2: Principles of Perfect Practice

Competency: Go beyond basic mastery of skills to expand your learning

Tool: *Principles of Perfect Practice*

EXCELLENCE WITH INTEGRITY

PRINCIPLES OF PERFECT PRACTICE

1. Practice with focus:
- » Focus on growth and improvement of existing skills.
- » Focus on adding new skills and developing deficient skills.

2. Practice with intensity:
- » Make practice more challenging than the 'real' challenge.
- » Deliberately design and monitor quality practice. Avoid just going through the motions.

3. Practice with consistency:
- » Devote consistent time to required practice. Don't binge and cram.

4. Practice with persistence.
- » Stay with it. Don't quit. Believe in yourself and the process.

© 2016 Institute for Excellence & Ethics (IEE)   www.excellenceand=thics.org

Objective

Students will use the Principles of Perfect Practice to enhance the skills needed to go beyond basic mastery and to expand learning.

Overview

1. Students will participate in a group discussion to identify the elements of perfect practice.

2. Students will engage in an Other-Study of Apolo Ohno to identify the elements of perfect practice.

3. Students will participate in the Drawing Challenge activity and establish a perfect practice routine based on the Principles of Perfect Practice.

Preparation

1. Determine how you will establish the behavioral norms needed to ensure a positive and productive learning experience for all students.

2. Cut the Draw Your Challenge Cards apart so that each student can choose a Draw Your Challenge Card.

3. Determine time allocations for drawing, plan development (in groups), presentation, etc.

4. Prepare external streaming video content:

   a. Review IEE policy regarding use of external content.

   b. "Apolo Ohno – KOMO News 'It's the biggest challenge of my life' "

      https://www.youtube.com/watch?v=c-j2G2a0Yko.

Materials

- Draw Your Challenge Cards (1 card for each student).
- Drawing supplies: paper, colored pencils, markers, etc.
- Optional: Sheet of blank paper for full page drawings.

Module Delivery Steps

Introduction:

1. Begin the lesson by displaying the following quote from Vince Lombardi: "*Practice does not make perfect. Only perfect practice makes perfect.*"

2. Facilitate a discussion on the meaning of the quote.

   ◊ *Vince Lombardi was the head football coach of the Green Bay Packers from 1959-1967. During that time, his Packer teams were famous for running the "Packer Sweep," a play that was fairly simple, and that everyone knew they were going to run consistently. In fact, the reason why their opponents understood the play so well was because Lombardi would often diagram the play for opposing coaches and television cameras. Why would he do such a thing? Because his philosophy was that if his team worked hard for "perfect practice," even if the opposing team knew the play was coming, they still would not be able to stop it. How did his philosophy work? In his 9 seasons as head coach in Green Bay, the Packers won 5 league championships, including the first two Super Bowls ever played.*

   ◊ *So, what do you think are some of the elements of "perfect practice"?*

   ◊ *How much time do you think it takes to "get good" at something?* (The answer, based on information from *Outliers* (Gladwell, 2008), is revealed at the end of the lesson.)

Guided Practice:

3. Introduce the Principles of Perfect Practice.

   ◊ *One of the elements of the Habits for Excellence is "Practice with focus, intensity, & consistency." The Principles of Perfect Practice provides a structure to understand what exactly that entails.*

     » *First, we must practice with focus by concentrating on growth and improvement of our existing skills, but also focusing on adding new skills and developing deficient ones. We have to practice not only the things we like, but also the things that don't come easily and that we're not good at.*

     » *Second, we have to practice with intensity by making our practice more challenging than our "real" challenge. This requires that we deliberately design and monitor the quality of our practice.*

» *Third, it's critical to practice with consistency, by devoting consistent blocks of time, as opposed to neglecting practice for long periods of time, then trying to binge and cram.*

» *Fourth, we have to practice with persistence. It takes months and years to truly improve at something, not hours and days. We have to stay with it and believe in ourselves and the process.*

⊘ EXCELLENCE WITH INTEGRITY

PRINCIPLES OF PERFECT PRACTICE

1. Practice with focus:
» Focus on growth and improvement of existing skills.
» Focus on adding new skills and developing deficient skills.

2. Practice with intensity:
» Make practice more challenging than the 'real' challenge.
» Deliberately design and monitor quality practice. Avoid just going through the motions.

3. Practice with consistency:
» Devote consistent time to required practice. Don't binge and cram.

4. Practice with persistence.
» Stay with it. Don't quit. Believe in yourself and the process.

© 2016 Institute for Excellence & Ethics (IEE)   www.excellenceandethics.org

---

4.   Conduct the Apolo Ohno Other-Study (# 1 in the Student Workbook).

"Apolo Ohno – KOMO News 'It's the biggest challenge of my life' "

https://www.youtube.com/watch?v=c-j2G2a0Yko

5. Facilitate a discussion on the evidence students identified when watching the other-study. Replicate the chart on the board and record the evidence identified by the students. Discussion prompts:

    ◊   *What evidence did you see and hear that demonstrated the principle of practice with focus?*

    (Possible answers include: Apolo demonstrates each intricate move of his skate and then says, "It's automatic."; Apolo says, "I know why I'm doing this every day."; Reporter says, "He's an intense competitor. He's trying to lose 10 pounds and have the strongest legs of any skater.")

    ◊   *What evidence did you see and hear that demonstrated the principle of practice with intensity?*

    (Possible answers include: Apolo indicates there's a lot of yelling at practice; All aspects of his workout; Apolo says, "I'm hungry.")

    ◊   *What evidence did you see and hear that demonstrated the principle of practice with consistency?*

    (Possible answers include: "I've been doing this 6-12 hours a day for the past 12 years.")

    ◊   *What evidence did you see and hear that demonstrated the principle of practice with persistence?*

    (Possible answers include: Champions are made when no one is looking; examples in the workout. Having the long range goal in mind; working hard now to achieve success in the future.)

6. Introduce the Draw Your Challenge activity. Determine what drawing tools you will allow, e.g., markers, pencil only, etc. Include your parameters in the explanation of the task. The explanation may sound something like this:

    ◊   *We're now going to do an activity that might seem unrelated at first to what we've been talking about, but will help us learn how to develop a plan that puts the Principles of Perfect Practice into action. The activity is called Draw Your Challenge. Each of you will randomly choose a card which contains a word or phrase. Your task is to draw a picture that creates a visual interpretation of the word or phrase on your card (#2 in the Student Workbook).*

    ◊   *Here is an example: Frustrated*

◊   *You'll have _____ minutes to create your drawing, and upon com-pletion, everyone will present their drawing to the group.*

7.   Facilitate a presentation of the drawings. As students share, ask ques-tions related to the Principles of Perfect Practice:

◊   *In order to become proficient at the Draw Your Challenge activity:*

»   *Which of your skills would need improvement?*

»   *What new skills would be needed?*

»   *How much practice do you think it would take to be able to com-pete at a high level in the Draw Your Challenge activity?*

8.   Divide students into teams for this part of the lesson. Have teams com-plete #3 in the Student Workbook in which they need to develop a prac-tice routine that would lead to improved performance in the Draw Your Challenge activity.

9.   Have teams share their practice routines. As teams share, allow peers to give feedback, including constructive critique, to each group.

Closure & Assessment:

10.   Ask students to answer the questions in #4 in the Student Workbook.

11.   Conduct whole-class discussion by presenting the answers to the ques-tions, then expanding on the information with follow-up questions.

1.   *The answer is **False**. To date, scientists have not found specific genes that identify particular talents. They may someday, but right now scientists are unable to identify specific talent or in-nate ability that allows top performers to achieve greatness more easily than the average person. It is false to assume that you could be born a natural brain surgeon, skater, musician, or computer programmer.*

2.   *The answer is **c**. Studies of outstanding achievers, including concert pianists, sculptors, Olympic swimmers, world-class ten-nis players, mathematicians, and research neurologists, showed that most were not remarkable as children and didn't show su-perior talent. Typically, their extraordinary accomplishments oc-*

curred later in their adult lives and were fueled by strong motivation, commitment, and a network of support.

3. *The answer is **b**. In study after study of composers, basketball players, fiction writers, ice-skaters, concert pianists, chess players, and people who perform other complex tasks, 10,000 hours is the best estimate of practice hours required for true expertise. 10,000 hours is roughly equivalent to three hours a day, or 20 hours a week, of practice ... for over 10 years! It appears to take the brain this long to assimilate all that it needs to know to achieve true mastery. You can learn more about the 10,000 hour rule in* Outliers *(Gladwell, 2008).*

12.   Leave students with some final thoughts about Perfect Practice.

◊ *"Deliberate practice" is the term that is used in the research. The Principles of Perfect Practice provide a structure for thinking about how we establish a practice regimen, like Apolo's, which we can use as we strive to maximize our potential for excellence, not just in Olympic speed skating, but in all different areas.*

13.   Finish by having students complete a final Self-Study, #5 in the Student Workbook, asking them to reflect on how they can use the Principles of Perfect Practice in an area of their choice.

Extension:

14.   **Other-Study:** Identify examples of individuals and organizations that exemplify a commitment to deliberate practice. Study the following video by author Geoff Colvin, which draws upon his book, *Talent is Overrated*, and examines the role of deliberate practice in the workplace: https://www.youtube.com/watch?v=fVjkPJynEDs.

15.   **Self-Study:** Have students identify an area for improvement (e.g., a skill, or talent, they are trying to develop, an academic subject, a social skill, etc.) and establish a practice regimen based on the Principles of Perfect Practice.

16.   **Performance/Simulation:** Have students act out mock-interviews where one student plays an interviewer who is out to do a story on someone (another student) who has reached a high level of achievement by putting the Principles of Perfect Practice into action. Encourage students to be creative when developing their characters and writing a script for the mock-interview.

17. **Support & Challenge:** Set students up with a partner, either in or outside of the class, who could help encourage and monitor their Perfect Practice plan. As improvements are made, host celebrations and allow students to share the actual practice routines they used to improve their chosen skill.

"Draw Your Challenge" Cards

Make enough copies of the cards below so each student has their own card. Cut the cards and have students randomly choose their challenge. Or, create your own Challenge Cards based on the students in your class and their most likely challenges.

Trouble Lurking	No Time	Teamwork
Keeping a Secret	Danger Ahead	Sacrifice
No Way Out	Annoyance	In the Storm

Trouble Lurking	No Time	Teamwork
Keeping a Secret	Danger Ahead	Sacrifice
No Way Out	Annoyance	In the Storm

Trouble Lurking	No Time	Teamwork
Keeping a Secret	Danger Ahead	Sacrifice
No Way Out	Annoyance	In the Storm

Planning and Reflection

Module 3-3: The Mindset of Motivation

Competency: Commit to hard work and motivate yourself when things are not easy

Tool: *Mindset of Motivation Essentials*

EXCELLENCE WITH INTEGRITY

MINDSET OF MOTIVATION ESSENTIALS
TO ENHANCE WILLPOWER & GRIT

1. Focus on your **end-goals**.
   » Push past what is inconvenient or uncomfortable by keeping your end-goals in mind.

2. Focus on what you **can control**.
   » No matter what the challenge or situation, you get to choose how to respond.

3. Focus on **growth** and **improvement**.
   » Break your overall goal into smaller sub-goals in order to track your progress.
   » Learn from failures and setbacks; keep moving; keep improving.

© 2016 Institute for Excellence & Ethics (IEE)   www.excellenceandethics.org

---

Objective

Students will use the Mindset of Motivation Essentials to understand how to find the will to start and the grit to stick with it.

Overview

1. Students will participate in an Other-Study activity to identify the Mindset of Motivation Essentials in action.

2. Students will create their own "future story" (Payne, 2009).

3. Students will share their future stories in a Public Presentation.

Preparation

1. Determine how you will establish the behavioral norms needed to ensure a positive and productive learning experience for all students.

2. Determine amount of time students will get to create their future story.

3. Determine your facilitation procedures for the Public Presentation of future stories.

4. Prepare external streaming video content:

    a. Review IEE policy regarding use of external content.

    b. "Life Underground Still Hopeful for Chilean Miners"

    http://www.nbcnews.com/video/nightly-news/39350942#39350942.

Module Delivery Steps

Introduction:

1. Introduce the Mindset of Motivation Essentials.

⊘ EXCELLENCE *WITH* INTEGRITY

MINDSET OF MOTIVATION ESSENTIALS
TO ENHANCE WILLPOWER & GRIT

1. Focus on your **end-goals**.

» **Push past what is inconvenient or uncomfortable by keeping your end-goals in mind.**

2. Focus on what you **can control**.

» **No matter what the challenge or situation, you get to choose how to respond.**

3. Focus on **growth** and **improvement**.

» **Break your overall goal into smaller sub-goals in order to track your progress.**

» **Learn from failures and setbacks; keep moving; keep improving.**

www.excellenceandethics.org

◊ *The second habit of the Habits for Excellence highlights the need to "find the will to start and the grit to continue." This habit speaks to the mindset of motivation that is needed in order to realize our potential for excellence. Will, which is the shorthand term for willpower, speaks of the internal motivation that drives a person toward their goals. Grit is a term that refers to a person's diligence, persistence, and overall mental tenacity, or toughness, in pursuing their goals.*

◊ *We often think that motivation is something that one is born with. While it's true that some people by personality tend to be more goal-driven, research on motivation has identified three essential factors behind what enhances motivation: a sense of purpose, independence, and competence.*

◊ *The Mindset of Motivation Essentials distills the research down into three essentials that contribute to a mindset that enhances willpower and grit.*

» *First, the Mindset of Motivation requires us to focus on our end-goals. People become de-motivated when they forget or lose sight of the overall purpose. When we keep our eye on the desired end-goals, we're able to demonstrate willpower and grit as we push past things that are difficult, inconvenient, and uncomfortable.*

» *Second, the Mindset of Motivation requires us to take ownership of our destiny by focusing on what we can control. People become de-motivated when they begin to feel that they have no control of their situation. We sometimes call this the "Have to/ Get to Switch": when we realize that no matter what the challenge or situation, we still get to choose how we'll respond. We don't have to do anything—except, as the saying goes, "die and pay taxes"—and we even don't have to pay taxes if we don't mind going to jail, and even if we are in jail, we still get to choose how we'll respond.*

» *Finally, the Mindset of Motivation requires you to focus on growth and improvement. People get de-motivated when they feel that their abilities are fixed, set, or unchangeable, or when they feel the challenge is just too great. Breaking the challenge down into smaller sub-goals and then focusing on moving forward and improving is the key.*

2. Conduct an Other-Study using the NBC News video of the 33 Chilean miners trapped in a mine more than 2,000 feet below the earth's surface (#1 in the Student Workbook).

◊ *On August 5, 2010, 33 Chilean miners became trapped over 2,000 feet underground. At the time of this video, the miners had been trapped for seven weeks:*

http://www.nbcnews.com/video/nightly-news/39350942#39350942

3. Facilitate a discussion that prompts students to make connections between the behaviors exhibited by the miners and the Mindset of Motivation. Possible connections may include:

◊ *What is the end-goal that the miners stay focused on and how does it help them push past what is difficult, uncomfortable, or inconvenient?*

Possible answers: The prize/end goal is to (short-term) make it through the day and eventually (long-term) make it out of the mine alive.

◊ *How do the miners focus on what they can control?*

Possible answers: They help the rescue workers by clearing rock and alerting the team above ground as to what is happening with the drilling; keeping fit through exercise.

◊ *How are the miners breaking their end-goal into sub-goals?*

Possible answers: Creating a schedule of day and night to get through each day; working; media training.

Guided Practice:

4. To begin the main learning experience, explain to students that they will be writing a story about their future and connecting their future story with the Mindset of Motivation Essentials. Introduction to the activity may sound something like this:

    ◊ *There are three common life experiences where having the Mindset of Motivation is essential for mustering up the willpower and grit needed to overcome challenges and reach your performance goals:*

    » *Extraordinary life circumstances or tragedies — such as serious illness, or something like the miners are experiencing.*

    » *Personal challenges or limitations — such as overcoming a physical or learning challenge, improving at something you're not naturally good at, learning a new skill/talent, getting in healthier shape, learning a new language, etc.*

    » *Grind of everyday life challenges — such as overcoming boredom, fatigue, doing what you don't want to do when you don't want to do it, etc.*

    ◊ *The story about the miners is certainly an inspirational story; however, it is an extraordinary life circumstance, which makes it difficult for us to relate to their experience. In order to better understand how the Mindset of Motivation Essentials can be beneficial on a daily basis, this activity is closer to our own current reality.*

◊ *The activity we are going to do today was developed as a result of research conducted on why some students are motivated and others aren't.*

◊ *You're going to work on creating a "Future Story" (#2 in the Student Workbook). A future story is a vision for your future. Without it, neither schooling nor work has much purpose or significance. That doesn't mean you have to have your entire life figured out, most people never really do, but it does mean that you should think about how you want your future story to turn out in order to begin moving in that direction.*

◊ *Use the prompts in the Student Workbook to write your future story. After you write your future story, use the prompts to begin thinking about how to use the Mindset of Motivation Essentials in order to find the willpower and grit to keep your story moving. We will share our future stories with the whole group.*

5.   After the students have had ample time to write their future story and connect the story elements to the Mindset of Motivation Essentials, allow students to share their future stories. When students are sharing, focus on providing Support & Challenge opportunities.

Closure & Assessment:

6.   Ask students to share their reactions to the following question:

◊ *Which is better: To give it your all and fail, or to fail having given very little effort?*

Possible follow-up comments:

◊ *The big danger of not working hard is that it robs us of all our excuses. If we haven't really given our best, we can always say, "Oh, I could have done that if I had really wanted to work at it."*

◊ *It's not easy to admit, but our fear of failure often prevents us from trying hard and really giving the sustained effort needed to improve.*

◊ *The fear of trying hard relates to our mindset about talent. If we think a person is born "talented," then we think they probably don't have to work as hard as we do to succeed, so we try to look for something else we might be better at. But remember, talent isn't fixed; it grows through practice, effort, and coaching.*

(Dweck, 2006)

7.   Close the lesson by reviewing and reinforcing the usefulness of the Mindset of Motivation Essentials. Closing may sound something like this:

> ◊   *When it comes to motivation, there's no question that "it's an inside job." It's very difficult for someone else to effectively and consistently motivate you. You have to find ways to motivate yourself.*

> ◊   *As we discussed today, motivation comes from a specific kind of mindset. You motivate yourself by a belief in and desire for improvement; by a belief that you get to choose how you will approach a task; and by a belief in and desire for your end-goal. No matter what you want to accomplish in the future, it will require the will to start and the grit to continue. If you develop the Mindset of Motivation, these essentials will help you overcome extraordinary life circumstances, personal obstacles, and the grind of everyday life.*

Extension:

8.   **Self-Study:** Have students create a Do-It-Yourself (DIY) Report Card (Pink, 2009, p. 177). At the beginning of the term, have students list their top learning goals. Then, at the end of the semester, ask them to review their progress. Where did they succeed? Where did they fall short? What more do they need to learn?

9.   **Performance/Simulation:** Have students create a "What Motivates You?" public service announcement campaign. This project could consist of anything from simply jotting down ideas of what the campaign might entail, to actually shooting and editing video clips, or to whatever other creative level you and your students take it to!

10.   **Support & Challenge:** As students are working on their learning goals (DIY report cards), meet with them individually to review how they are doing and what support they might need.

11.   **Other-Study:** Have students find a "Future Story Mentor" that will be able to give them tips and perhaps even experiences that can help them turn their Future Story from fiction to reality. Meet with students individually to counsel them on the selection of their mentor. You can also discuss with the class the guidelines for what interactions between student and mentor should take place.

Planning and Reflection

4. Building on Strengths and Passion

Module 4-1: Character SWOT Analysis

Competency: Know your character strengths and weaknesses

Tool: *Character SWOT Analysis*

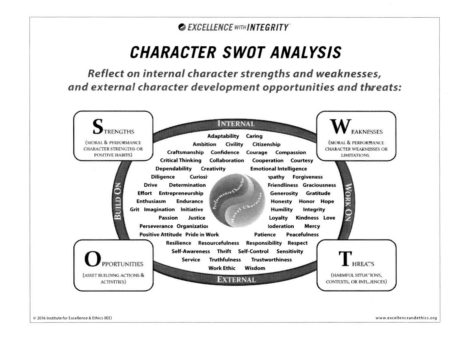

Objective

Students will use the Character SWOT Analysis to identify their character strengths and weaknesses.

Overview

1. Students will complete the Character SWOT Analysis.

2. Students will share their identified strengths, weaknesses, opportunities, and threats with a partner and identify a person who can Support & Challenge them.

Preparation

1. Determine how you will establish the behavioral norms needed to ensure a positive and productive learning experience for all students.

2. Determine pacing for Character SWOT Analysis activity.

Module Delivery Steps

Introduction:

1.   Begin today's lesson by posing the following question to students. Allow students time to think and reflect silently in writing about their response.

     ◊   *Explain what it means to say: "Character is power."*

2.   Facilitate a class discussion, allowing students to share their responses.

     ◊   *In the Excellence with Integrity framework character is defined as "values in action." We know that someone is honest, hard working, or trustworthy when they put those values into action.*

⊘ EXCELLENCE *WITH* **INTEGRITY**

VALUES MAP

Adaptability   Caring

Ambition   Civility   Citizenship

Craftsmanship   Confidence   Courage   Compassion

Critical Thinking   Collaboration   Cooperation   Courtesy

Dependability   Creativity   Emotional Intelligence

Diligence   Curiosi͟   ͟pathy   Forgiveness

Drive   Determination   Friendliness   Graciousness

Effort   Entrepreneurship   Generosity   Gratitude

Enthusiasm   Endurance   Honesty   Honor   Hope

Grit   Imagination   Initiative   Humility   Integrity

Passion   Justice   Loyalty   Kindness   Love

Perseverance   Organizatio͟   ͟loderation   Mercy

Positive Attitude   Pride in Work   Patience   Peacefulness

Resilience   Resourcefulness   Responsibility   Respect

Self-Awareness   Thrift   Self-Control   Sensitivity

Service   Truthfulness   Trustworthiness

Work Ethic   Wisdom

Adapted from Lickona & Davidson (2005).

© 2016 Institute for Excellence & Ethics (IEE)   www.excellenceandethics.org

---

3.   Introduce the concepts of Performance Character and Moral Character.

◊ *Excellence with Integrity framework is based on a two-part theory of character: performance character and moral character.*

◊ *Performance character consists of those values in action—such as effort, self-discipline, and perseverance—that enable us to do our best in any performance environment.*

◊ *If someone puts these values into action they have extra power to perform, as compared to someone with equal ability who does not use these values.*

◊ *It's performance character that helps us maximize our potential for excellence—in school, work, sports, music, drama, or any other endeavor.*

◊ *Moral character refers to those values needed for successful relationships and ethical behavior such as fairness, honesty, respect, and humility.*

◊ *It's our moral character that ensures that we don't lie, cheat, steal, or take unethical shortcuts in pursuit of our goals.*

◊ *Character becomes power when we put performance character values and moral character values into action.*

4.   Have students discuss the following prompt with a partner:

◊ *Sometimes it's easier to think about big ideas, like the idea of character as power, by thinking about people and experiences in your own life. With your partner, describe a person or experience from your life that demonstrates the power of character.*

5.   Discuss the responses shared among partners as a whole group.

6.   Help students understand the connections between character and talent by explaining that talent is what you are born with and character is what you do with your talent.

Guided Practice:

7.   Introduce the Character SWOT Analysis.

◊ *The Character SWOT Analysis assists us in evaluating the current state of our internal and external character strengths and weaknesses.*

◊ *SWOT stands for Strengths, Weaknesses, Opportunities and Threats.*

◊ *Strengths are internal elements of our character that we can build on, while weaknesses are internal elements that we need to work on.*

◊ *Opportunities are external actions and activities that we can build on, while threats are external contexts, settings, or influences that we need to work on (or maybe even avoid altogether).*

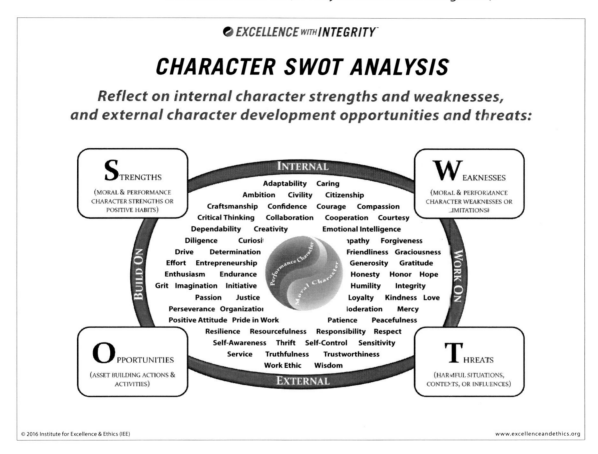

8. Introduce the Character SWOT Analysis activity.

◊ *We will begin today's activity by evaluating the current state of your personal character strengths and weaknesses.*

◊ *In your Student Workbook, first list the strengths: Moral & Performance Character strengths or positive habits—values that really epitomize who you are, those you go to when you are in need. For example, is it your honesty, your work ethic, your courage?*

◊ *Then identify your weaknesses: Moral & Performance Character weaknesses or limitations—values you'd like to develop to a higher degree, values that can cause you problems if you don't watch them. For example, maybe you'd like to be more honest, or maybe you struggle with your attitude, or tend not to be as responsible for work as you should be.*

9.   Provide students with sufficient time to reflect and complete the first portion of the SWOT Analysis. When students are ready, continue with the activity.

◊   *There are always opportunities available to help positively develop your character; it's just that we don't always recognize them as opportunities. Each of the opportunities provides the chance to develop a new and different character muscle. Some may be easy for you; others may be a real challenge.*

◊   *Use this list to brainstorm some opportunities you'd like to take advantage of. In particular look for opportunities that may help you build one of the character weaknesses you identified earlier.*

10. Continue with the final component of the SWOT analysis.

◊   *Character development threats are frequently present. There are lots of ways that poor habits, bad decisions, and the wrong friends can threaten your character. Just because threats exist, doesn't mean we will fall prey to them. But the more we are aware of our threats, the more likely we are to avoid them.*

◊   *Brainstorm some character development threats that you want to avoid. In particular look for threats that you might be particularly vulnerable to because of character weaknesses you identified. Write these threats down in your Student Workbook.*

11. Continue by providing an opportunity for students to share their SWOT Analysis with a partner. Explain the directions for the partner-share:

◊   *Share the strengths, weaknesses, opportunities, and threats you identified, then identify someone who can Support and Challenge you to build on your strengths and opportunities, while working on your weaknesses and threats. After you have finished your discussion, write the name of the person you identified in your Student Workbook.*

Closure & Assessment:

12. Close the lesson by reviewing the Character SWOT Analysis and its importance. Closing comments might begin like this:

    ◊ *The Character SWOT Analysis is a strategic self-reflection tool used to identify your character strengths and weaknesses, and character development opportunities and threats.*

    ◊ *While you are responsible for developing your character, your environment also acts to shape and build your character. The groups to which you belong—your home, school, friends, extra-curricular activities—all influence your character development. Your environment provides opportunities for your character development, and it also provides threats to your character development. The Character SWOT Analysis is a powerful continuous improvement tool.*

Extension:

13. **Other-Study:** Have students look for examples of individuals who demonstrate the same character strengths they have personally identified as areas for improvement. For example, if positive attitude was identified as area for improvement, the student can seek to identify individuals who demonstrate positive attitude and describe how they do so, then create a list of habits to model and practice.

14. **Self-Study:** Have students create a plan to monitor the development of one of the values identified as a weakness, checking in on progress at strategic times (i.e., each day, each week, etc.).

15. **Performance/Simulation:** Have students share aloud what strengths, weaknesses, opportunities, and threats they identified, and how they plan to use the Character SWOT Tool to improve their moral and performance character.

16. **Support & Challenge:** Have students keep a SWOT Support & Challenge Journal to track communication with the person they have identified. Encourage students to speak or meet with this accountability partner at least once per week and summarize their check-ins as well as their actions between meetings.

Planning and Reflection

Module 4-2: Elevator Speech

Competency: Communicate your passion and perspective in a concise and memorable way

Tool: *Elevator Speech Essentials and Habits for Excellence Personal Profile*

● EXCELLENCE WITH INTEGRITY

ELEVATOR SPEECH ESSENTIALS

Harness your knowledge, experience, passion, and plans in a 'sticky' story that is:

» **Concise**

» **Credible**

» **Relevant**

» **Emotional**

» **Memorable**

Adapted from Heath & Heath (2007).

www.excellnceandethics.org

● EXCELLENCE WITH INTEGRITY

HABITS FOR EXCELLENCE PERSONAL PROFILE

Please indicate how closely the statements below reflect your own attitudes and beliefs.	Not true for me	Sort of true for me	Defin'tely true for me
1. I believe that through hard work I can improve at most anything.			
2. I believe that natural ability is the most important factor in determining success.			
3. I worry about how my abilities compare to those of others.			
4. I am afraid of failure.			
5. I am always looking for ways to improve.			
6. I often struggle to motivate myself to work harder.			
7. I look for challenges and opportunities that test and stretch my abilities.			
8. I often settle for "good enough."			
9. I believe you've either got ability or you don't, and that no amount of practice can change that.			
10. I am able to make myself practice to improve skills that I am not good at.			
11. I am able to take constructive criticism and advice and use it to improve.			
12. I am able to work hard on my own to improve my skills and abilities.			
13. I am able to engage in intense and concentrated practice for extended periods of time.			
14. I am able to practice a skill over and over until I have it mastered.			
15. I am able to make myself practice to improve at things I don't like.			

www.excellenceandethics.org

Objective

Students will use the sample Habits for Excellence Personal Profile to practice creating an Elevator Speech.

Overview

1. Students will complete the Habits for Excellence Personal Profile.
2. Students will use the Habits for Excellence sample profile to create an Elevator Speech.

Preparation

1. Determine how you will establish the behavioral norms needed to ensure a positive and productive learning experience for all students.
2. Determine the time allotted for drafting of Elevator Speeches.
3. Determine method, timing, and scoring procedure for Elevator Speech presentations.
4. Prepare external streaming video content:
   a. Review IEE policy regarding use of external content.
   b. "Elevator Speech - Cassie"
      http://www.teachertube.com/video/elevator-speech-cassie-198438
   c. "Elevator Speech - Teresa"
      http://www.teachertube.com/video/elevator-speech-teresa-198439
   d. "The Pursuit of Happyness - Job Interview"
      https://www.youtube.com/watch?v=qbcj2WM7mNs
      Note: Strong language is used beginning just after 3:40; determine video use accordingly.

Module Delivery Steps

Introduction:

1.   Introduce the Elevator Speech Essentials.

⊘ *EXCELLENCE WITH INTEGRITY*

ELEVATOR SPEECH ESSENTIALS

Harness your knowledge, experience, passion, and plans in a 'sticky' story that is:

- » **Concise**
- » **Credible**
- » **Relevant**
- » **Emotional**
- » **Memorable**

Adapted from Heath & Heath (2007).

    www.excellenceandethics.org

◊ *Interviews are great opportunities to showcase your talents and potential for success. However, interviews are not the only opportunity to create and deliver a persuasive pitch demonstrating your potential for success. Often we are presented with brief and unexpected opportunities to share who we are and what we would like to do.*

◊ *An Elevator Speech is a brief statement about yourself, prepped and ready for use at a moment's notice should you ever find yourself on an elevator ride, or having another brief interaction, with a person of influence. Since, as the saying goes, "you only have one chance to make a good first impression," an Elevator Speech is something you need to prepare and practice to deliver it well.*

◊ *A good Elevator Speech is concise, credible, relevant, emotional, and memorable.*

» *It's concise — it usually lasts anywhere from 30 seconds up to 2 minutes.*

» *It's credible — it must be accurate and believable.*

» *It's relevant — you're talking about things that are to the point and matter to the person you're speaking with.*

» *It's emotional — you're not weeping all over them, but you've got to make the person listening care about you and your story.*

» *It's memorable – it's not cheesy or annoying, but it is unique and interesting.*

2.   Continue by having students view the following Elevator Speech examples and take notes in #1 in the Student Workbook.

"Elevator Speech – Cassie"
http://www.teachertube.com/video/elevator-speech-cassie-198438

"Elevator Speech – Teresa"
http://www.teachertube.com/video/elevator-speech-teresa-198439

3.   Finish the introduction by having students discuss the outcomes they found as they viewed the two elevator speech examples.

◊ *Were the examples concise?*

◊ *Were the examples credible?*

◊ *Were the examples relevant?*

◊ *Were the examples emotional?*

◊ *Were the examples memorable?*

Guided Practice:

4.   Continue by having students reflect upon their own areas of strength, and upon areas to improve using the Habits for Excellence Personal Profile.

EXCELLENCE WITH INTEGRITY

HABITS FOR EXCELLENCE PERSONAL PROFILE

Please indicate how closely the statements below reflect your own attitudes and beliefs.	Not true for me	Sort of true for me	Definitely true for me
1. I believe that through hard work I can improve at most anything.			
2. I believe that natural ability is the most important factor in determining success.			
3. I worry about how my abilities compare to those of others.			
4. I am afraid of failure.			
5. I am always looking for ways to improve.			
6. I often struggle to motivate myself to work harder.			
7. I look for challenges and opportunities that test and stretch my abilities.			
8. I often settle for "good enough."			
9. I believe you've either got ability or you don't, and that no amount of practice can change that.			
10. I am able to make myself practice to improve skills that I am not good at.			
11. I am able to take constructive criticism and advice and use it to improve.			
12. I am able to work hard on my own to improve my skills and abilities.			
13. I am able to engage in intense and concentrated practice for extended periods of time.			
14. I am able to practice a skill over and over until I have it mastered.			
15. I am able to make myself practice to improve at things I don't like.			

www.excellenceandethics.org

◊ As you begin to think about preparing for college or job interviews, internships, or work apprenticeship opportunities, it will be important for you to be able to identify areas of strength, as well as areas to improve upon.

◊ This Personal Profile provides a self-reflection for benchmarking your Habits for Excellence beliefs and behaviors. There are no right or wrong answers; this Profile is simply meant to assist you in identifying areas of strength to build upon, and areas of growth for improving, so assess your current beliefs and behaviors honestly.

◊ Complete the Habits for Excellence Personal Profile (# 2 in the Student Workbook). As you complete the Profile, think about how you are generally, not just with things you like or are good at, or just things you don't like or struggle with.

5. After completing the Habits for Excellence Personal Profile, as a class discuss how the knowledge from the Personal Profile could be useful during the creation of a Elevator Speech (#3 in the Student Workbook).

6. Continue by explaining to students the activity for the creation of Elevator Speech (#4 in the Student Workbook). In order to focus the activity, all students will use a prepared Sample Profile when developing the elevator speech. Explanation may sound something like this:

   ◊ *Here's the scenario: You have applied for a program you really want to get into; it could be a job, college, internship or other type of program. Many others have also applied. The individuals reviewing the applications have asked that you come in and deliver a two-minute speech designed to separate yourself from the other applicants and to convince them of your potential for success in the program.*

   ◊ *They have already reviewed your other performance measures, as well as your Habits for Excellence Profile, but now they want to hear from you. Remember that they will also be hearing from the other applicants, so you must develop and deliver a powerful speech, if you hope to distinguish yourself.*

   ◊ *Here are the rules of the Habits for Excellence Elevator Speech Challenge:*

   ◊ *You will work with a partner to create and deliver a concise, credible, relevant, emotional, memorable speech not more than two minutes long, using the Habits for Excellence Sample Profile provided for you. Your group's job is to persuade an interviewer that you have the most potential for success.*

   ◊ *For this challenge each group will present on the same Sample Profile (see #4 in the Student Workbook). Since the interviewer has already reviewed the Profile as part of the original application, your Elevator Speech should be sure to address both strengths and areas for improvement represented in the Profile to persuade them of your potential for excellence.*

   ◊ *Each Elevator Speech will be scored using the Elevator Speech Scoring rubric in #5 in the Student Workbook.*

7. Have students work with a partner to draft, rehearse, and revise their sample Elevator Speech.

8. Have students present their Elevator Speeches to the class. Use Scoring Rubric in #4 in the Student Workbook to discuss the presentations.

Closure & Assessment:

9.   Have students watch a video clip from the movie *The Pursuit of Happyness*. Introduction to the clip may sound something like this:

◊   *In this clip from the movie <u>The Pursuit of Happyness</u>, Chris Gardner, played by Will Smith, is given the opportunity to deliver something similar to an elevator speech. In the story, due to his unpaid parking tickets, he was removed from his home and taken to jail. As a result, he is late for the meeting for the stockbroker internship at the prestigious stock brokerage and securities firm, Dean Witter. As you watch, look for elements of the Elevator Speech: concise, credible, relevant, emotional, and memorable.*

"The Pursuit of Happyness – Job Interview"
https://www.youtube.com/watch?v=qbcj2WM7mNs

Note: Strong language is used beginning just after 3:40; determine video use accordingly.

10.   Close the lesson by having students create a first draft of their own Elevator Speech based on the results of their Habits for Excellence Personal Profile. Explanation may sound something like this:

◊   *What type of situation would you want to develop an Elevator Speech for? The objective of today's lesson was to introduce you to the Elevator Speech strategy; the development of a speech that communicates your potential for success in a way that is concise, credible, relevant, emotional, and memorable. You'll need to give thought to creating a powerful Elevator Speech, but you'll also need a starting point; a first draft you can work from.*

◊   *The final task in today's lesson is to develop a first draft of your own Elevator Speech based on your Habits for Excellence Personal Profile.*

◊   *As you draft your Elevator Speech, make sure that you present your story in a way that is concise, credible, relevant, emotional, and memorable.*

Extension:

11. **Other-Study:** Have students use the elements of the Elevator Speech to identify Other-Study examples of good elevator speeches found in movies. A Google Search of "Elevator Pitch" or "Elevator Speech" yields many good examples, including the following:

     https://www.youtube.com/watch?v=r_Dgsf4iiZg.

12. **Self-Study:** Have students develop their own Elevator Speech beyond a first draft and into a speech that represents an authentic demonstration of their understanding of the Elevator Speech concept. Encourage them to get feedback on the drafts of their Elevator Speech, revising throughout the process.

13. **Performance/Simulation:** Have students deliver their Elevator Speeches to their peers and/or community members (local professionals, college or career counselors, etc.).

14. **Support & Challenge:** Have students identify people who can help them develop a powerful Elevator Speech. Use the Capable Coaching Fundamentals to help students understand what qualities they should look for when seeking out individuals for Support & Challenge.

Planning and Reflection

Planning and Reflection

5. Managing Priorities and Stress

Module 5-1: Stress Management Process

Competency: Use productive strategies for reducing stress

Tools: *Stress Management Steps*

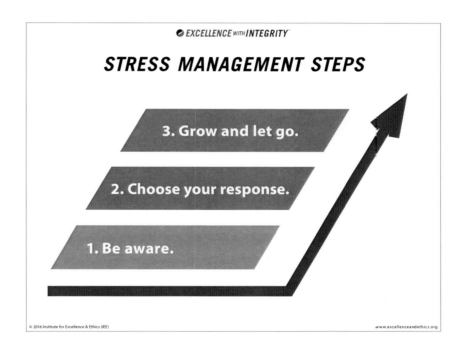

Objective

Students will use the Stress Management Steps to master productive strategies for reducing stress.

Overview

1. Students will participate in creating a Stress Management Pamphlet for younger students.

2. Students will identify strategies they currently use to cope with stress and will learn about productive strategies for managing and reducing stress.

3. Students will select and put into practice support and challenge practices for stress management.

Preparation

1. Determine how you will establish the behavioral norms needed to ensure a positive and productive learning experience for all students.

2. Determine how you will group students into the activity, and what template you will use (paper, digital, etc.) for students to create a Stress Management Pamphlet.

3. Prepare external streaming video content:

    a. Review IEE policy regarding use of external content.

    b. Choose video(s) you will use for this lesson:

        i. "Can You Feel It?"

            http://www.youtube.com/watch?v=LFkryxkAh5g

        ii. "The Single Most Important Thing You Can Do For Your Stress"

            https://www.youtube.com/watch?v=I6402QJp52M

        iii. "How to Make Stress Your Friend"

            https://www.youtube.com/watch?v=RcGyVTAoXEU

Materials

-   Template for Stress Management Pamphlet as determined above (an example is included in the Student Workbook).

Module Delivery Steps

Introduction:

1. Begin by having students reflect on the true/false statements in #1 in the Student Workbook.

2. Conduct a group discussion. Use the information below to discuss the prevalence of stress.

    ◊   *In fact, all of these statements are true. For more facts about the impact of stress go to* http://www.stress.org:

3. Share the following video introducing an overview of stress:

    https://www.youtube.com/watch?v=TZZlIKXcolo.

    Continue by asking students to identify what is meant by the terms "stress" and "stressor" (#2 in the Student Workbook). Clarify these concepts by using some of the information below.

    »   *Stress is your body's response to strain, tension, threat, or challenge. Stress can be physical, emotional, or mental.*

    »   *Your body's response can be physical (such as getting sweaty palms or goose bumps), mental (such as struggling to focus or concentrate), or emotional (such as feeling nervous or uptight).*

    »   *Sometimes stress is caused by big things like an important test, or the death of a loved one, or meeting someone for the first time. Other times stress comes from a bunch of seemingly little things that don't really matter, and yet somehow they come together in a perfect storm of stress.*

    »   *A stressor is anything that causes strain, tension, or challenge. Stressors vary depending on the individual, the situation, and lots of other factors.*

    »   *For example, at one point your parents can act as a stress reducer helping you to handle difficult decisions and providing you support to manage your commitments. But sometimes your parents can become a stressor if, for example, they have been on you about a particular issue.*

    »   *Your friends can be a source of great support helping reduce stress. But they can also be a stressor, if they're applying pressure on you to do something, or if you're simply not getting along.*

4. Take some time to allow students to brainstorm in partnerships different stressors in their life that result in increased level of stress (#3 in the Student Workbook). After an adequate amount of time has passed, allow students to share out the different stressors that they find most often lead to stress.

5. Introduce the Stress Management Steps:

    ◊   *As your challenges grow and your time becomes more limited, feeling stressed out can become an all too common experience. While you may not be able to avoid stress, you can learn to manage it.*

    ◊   *The Stress Management Steps offers three simple steps for managing stress:*

    1. *First, we have to be aware and understand what stress is, where it comes from, and how it impacts us. The causes and impact of stress are different for each of us, so first we have to learn what it is, where it comes from, and how it impacts each of us personally.*

    2. *Second, we have to choose how we will respond when we are faced with stressors. We do this by focusing on those things that are in our control. And by being willing to stop or change how we are responding to stress, once we see that our previous approach may not be working.*

    3. *Finally, we have to find ways to grow from our stress, and learn to let go of the things we can't control or do anything about. We need to focus on growth, not perception or perfection, and to let go of the past and the things we can't change.*

6. Share and discuss one or more of the following videos on stress and its impact on our mind and body. Discuss with student the ways in which stress can be positive and productive and how it can also be harmful. Finally, discuss what they see as the key things to think, believe, and do to manage stress effectively.

    "Can You Feel It?"

    http://www.youtube.com/watch?v=LFkryxkAh5g

    "The Single Most Important Thing You Can Do For Your Stress"

    https://www.youtube.com/watch?v=I6402QJp52M

    "How to Make Stress Your Friend"

    https://www.youtube.com/watch?v=RcGyVTAoXEU

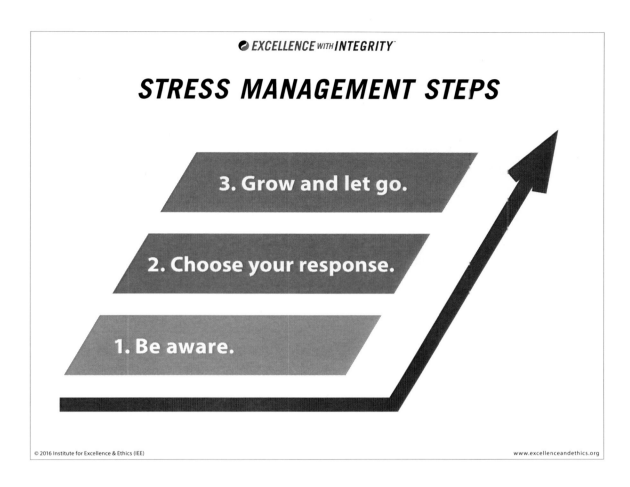

Guided Practice:

7.   Break students into groups of 3-4 for the remainder of the lesson.

8.   Introduce today's activity by explaining to students that they will be creating a Stress Management Pamphlet. Choose a target audience, for example, new students. Students will need to: (1) identify potential stressors that the target audience may encounter, (2) identify positive and productive strategies for managing the identified stressors, and (3) identify ways in which individuals may grow, or things they may learn to let go of from these stressful situations or experiences.

9.   Give students time to brainstorm different stressors that they have experienced.

10.   After an appropriate amount of time has passed for brainstorming, direct small groups to use either the template in #4 in the Student Work-

book, or a separate paper copy, or a digital template in the software of their choice. The completed template will become a Stress Management Pamphlet.

11. Explain to students the requirements for successful completion of the pamphlet (see #4 in the Student Workbook).

12. Discuss and post an example for students on the board to use as a model. You may want to use the following as a possible example:

◊ *Stressor: applying to college.*

◊ *Positive and Productive strategies for managing this stressor:*

» *(1) Start the process early.*

» *(2) Make a timeline that breaks the task into smaller parts. Include due dates for rough drafts and revisions.*

» *(3) Tell your plan to a parent or advisor so that they can help you stick to your timeline.*

◊ *How will you grow from this stressor: You will learn to manage tasks by breaking them into smaller pieces. You will practice the writing process.*

13. Remind students throughout the creation of the pamphlet to look back at the Stress Management Steps and to reflect upon the video other-studies as a guide.

14. Allow students a specified amount of time to present their Stress Management Pamphlets to the class.

Closure & Assessment:

15. Close the lesson by conducting a group discussion (see #5 in the Student Workbook): As a group, brainstorm strategies for how you can support and challenge one another as you strive to manage stress in productive and positive ways.

Extension:

16. **Other-Study:** Have students identify positive examples and counter-examples of the Stress Management Steps in literature, television, movies, music, and current events. Allow students to share the examples they find with the group, then, as a group, use the Stress Management Steps to discuss what elements are or are not present.

17. Self-Study: Have students keep a daily journal in which they reflect on how they are putting the Stress Management Steps into practice and if they are seeing any change in their levels of stress. Encourage students to be open and honest in their reflections. At the end of an assigned period of time (1 week, 2 weeks, etc.), give students an opportunity to read back over their journal entries and reflect on them collectively in some way (written response, partner or group sharing, one-on-one meetings with you, etc.).

18. **Performance/Simulation:** Have students extend the activity within the lesson by allowing students to present their Stress Management Pamphlets to various audiences.

19. **Support & Challenge:** Have students share the strategies they committed to putting into practice with a partner, a small group, or the entire class. Give students an opportunity to check back in at regular intervals (every day, every few days, once per week, etc.) to see if they are sticking with the strategies they identified. Encourage students to be open and honest, using check-ins as opportunities for continued growth.

Planning and Reflection

Module 5-2: Priorities and Time Management

Competency: Monitor, define, prioritize and complete tasks without direct oversight

Tool: *Time Management Troubleshooting Tips*

EXCELLENCE WITH INTEGRITY

TIME MANAGEMENT TROUBLESHOOTING TIPS

» **Know your limits.** We rarely regret saying, "No." But we often regret saying, "Yes."

» **Reflect to recover.** Reflect continuously on where your time goes. Recover lost and wasted time and recommit it to whatever matters most.

» **Multi-task with care.** It can help recover lost time, OR prevent the concentrated effort many tasks require.

» **Attack procrastination.** The best defense is a good offense: Do immediately the things you don't like or are worried about.

» **If you want more time, get more energy.** You'll be more positive and productive with healthy life habits like good nutrition, consistent exercise, rest, and rejuvenation.

© 2016 Institute for Excellence & Ethics (IEE) www.excellenceandethics.org

Objective

Students will use the Time Management Troubleshooting Tips to improve their time and task management habits.

Overview

1. Students will watch a video on procrastination and discuss its message.

2. Students will work in small groups to identify the main cause of each of the time-management dilemmas and identify specific tips.

3. Student groups will present their solutions to the entire class and scores will be given for identifying the main cause of the time-management dilemma and the specific tips provided.

Preparation

1. Determine how you will establish the behavioral norms needed to ensure a positive and productive learning experience for all students.

2. Establish a procedure for keeping score during the public presentation portion of activity.

3. Prepare external streaming video content:

    a. Review IEE policy regarding use of external content.

    b. "Tales of Mere Existence"by Lev Yilmaz:

      https://www.youtube.com/watch?v=4P785j15Tzk

      https://www.youtube.com/watch?v=Y9NgXIkyiwk.

Module Delivery Steps

Introduction:

1. Begin the lesson by discussing the following quote by Henry Ford and asking for reactions from students based their own experiences.

    "Most people spend more time and energy going around problems than in trying to solve them."

2. Continuing by sharing either or both of the following videos from the "Tales of Mere Existence" on procrastination and getting ready:

    https://www.youtube.com/watch?v=4P785j15Tzk

    https://www.youtube.com/watch?v=Y9NgXIkyiwk

3. Facilitate a discussion to debrief the video. Possible prompts to get started might include:

    ◊   *Well, it's pretty obvious that these clips are poking fun at a common time-management challenge—procrastination. What from your own past and/or current behavior or tendencies could you relate to in the video?*

    ◊   *In your opinion, is procrastination something that everyone does, or are there some people who never procrastinate?*

    ◊   *What, in your experience, are the best strategies for overcoming procrastination?*

Guided Practice:

4. Introduce the Time Management Troubleshooting Tips. Introduction to the tool may sound something like this :

    ◊   *If time is so precious, then why do we find so many ways to lose it, waste it, or spend it poorly? Just because we have an awareness of our time-management tendencies, and we have good time-management tools, we still may occasionally find ourselves in some time-management trouble; in fact, at some point EVERYBODY struggles to manage their time well. Because of this, it's important to be prepared with strategies to address some of the most common time-management problems, which is what the Time Management Troubleshooting Tips offers: You may need to look for ways to recover lost time—before class, at lunch, early in the morning, etc. You may need to reconsider your commitments. You may need to re-think your procrastination tendencies. Or you may simply need to refocus your time, before things become almost due, due, or overdue. The Time Management Troubleshooting Tips gives you five things to consider, when you find yourself losing the battle with time.*

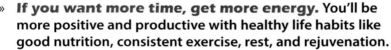

TIME MANAGEMENT TROUBLESHOOTING TIPS

» **Know your limits.** We rarely regret saying, "No." But we often regret saying, "Yes."

» **Reflect to recover.** Reflect continuously on where your time goes. Recover lost and wasted time and recommit it to whatever matters most.

» **Multi-task with care.** It can help recover lost time, OR prevent the concentrated effort many tasks require.

» **Attack procrastination.** The best defense is a good offense: Do immediately the things you don't like or are worried about.

» **If you want more time, get more energy.** You'll be more positive and productive with healthy life habits like good nutrition, consistent exercise, rest, and rejuvenation.

www.excellenceandethics.org

---

5.   Have students complete a Time Management Troubleshooting Tips Self-Study in #1 in the Student Workbook.

6.   Divide students into small groups/teams. The task is for each team to use the results from their personal self-studies above to conduct a team audit: based on personal experiences, what things would the team need to START, STOP, CONTINUE, and/or IMPROVE to put each tip into action more effectively (#2 in the Student Workbook).

Teams should brainstorm (encouraging everyone to contribute, aiming for productivity, and using active listening) and then organize, prioritize, and record their recommendations.

Note: Depending on time available, you can have different teams work on one tip, a couple of tips, or all five tips.

7. Have teams share their START, STOP, CONTINUE, and/or IMPROVE Audit recommendations.

Closure & Assessment:

8. Wrap up the activity by having students reflect on the fact that time is something that is truly limited. There are only so many hours in a day, only so many days in a week, and how we spend our time is how we spend our lives. But how we spend our time is in our control. Encourage students to share ideas for how they can work to overcome the struggle of implementing a new time-management strategy. Identify ways for the class to support each other throughout the year.

9. Have students complete the Self-Study reflection in #3 in the Student Workbook.

Extension:

10. **Other-Study**: Identify examples (and counter examples) of people who have found ways to work themselves out of time-management challenges. For example, have student leaders from senior classes visit your class during critical times of the year (e.g., preparation for mid-terms, finals, etc.) to share with students how they manage their time effectively. Have students determine which elements of the Time Management Troubleshooting Tips the student leaders put into action consistently. Search online for time-management videos like the following: https://www.youtube.com/watch?v=VUk6LXRZMMk.

11. **Self-Study**: When students state they "don't have enough time" to do things, like study, push their knowledge on a topic to a higher level, practice a skill, eat healthy, exercise, etc., have students use the Time

Management Troubleshooting Tips to identify the strategies they need to put into action in order to resolve their time-management issues (these could also be shared with a partner, teacher, mentor, class, etc. to add Performance/Simulation and Support & Challenge components).

12. **Performance/Simulation**: Provide students regular opportunities to share their time-management challenges to one another. (Presenting the challenges can be diagnostic for the presenter, provides important Other-Studies for ongoing reflection, and allows for the opportunity to have other students share possible strategies that address various time management challenges).

13. **Support & Challenge**: Using the Time Management Troubleshooting Tips as a guide, have students partner up with a time-management partner who can regularly provide support, as well as constructive critique, as students strive to manage their time well and work their way through the inevitable challenges. Develop a regular check-in time (e.g., every day, every Monday, once every other week, once per month, etc.) and check in with each group to ensure that experiences are being shared, feedback is being offered, and effective support and challenge is occurring.

Planning and Reflection

Planning and Reflection

6. Achieving Excellence with Integrity

Module 6-1: Rules of an Active Conscience

Competency: Develop an active conscience

Tool: *Rules of an Active Conscience*

⊘ EXCELLENCE WITH INTEGRITY

RULES OF AN ACTIVE CONSCIENCE

What NOT to do to keep your conscience as a guide for your integrity.

» **Don't distort.**
Don't exaggerate or blow things out of proportion.

» **Don't create an enemy.**
Don't avoid the truth by finding or creating an enemy to fight against.

» **Don't play the victim.**
Don't rationalize to convince self or others that I/we are really the victim.

» **Don't fan the flames.**
Don't get self/others fired-up so that emotion clouds reason.

» **Don't be a gamer.**
Don't try to convince self/others that it isn't wrong, "just how the game is played."

www.excellenceandethics.org

Objective

Students will use the Rules of an Active Conscience to understand and defend against conscience-quieting strategies.

Overview

1. Students will define conscience.

2. Students will conduct two Other-Studies showing Active and INactive Conscience.

3. Students will brainstorm and analyze typical examples that challenge integrity.

Preparation

1. Determine how you will establish the behavioral norms needed to ensure a positive and productive learning experience for all students.

2. Prepare external streaming video content:

   a. Review IEE policy regarding use of external content.

   b. "Lance Armstrong: After the Apology"

      https://www.youtube.com/watch?v=KQDmX5nVbVw.

   c. "1968 Summer Olympics, Black Power Salute"

      https://www.youtube.com/watch?v=qck5arjMGBg

Module Delivery Steps

Introduction:

1. Begin the lesson by asking students to discuss the following French proverb: *"There is no pillow so soft as a clear conscience."*

2. Continue by asking students to discuss with a partner the following question: *"What is conscience?"*

3. Introduce the Rules of an Active Conscience. Introduction of the tool might go something like this:

⊘ EXCELLENCE with INTEGRITY

RULES OF AN ACTIVE CONSCIENCE

What NOT to do to keep your conscience as a guide for your integrity.

» **Don't distort.**
   Don't exaggerate or blow things out of proportion.

» **Don't create an enemy.**
   Don't avoid the truth by finding or creating an enemy to fight against.

» **Don't play the victim.**
   Don't rationalize to convince self or others that I/we are really the victim.

» **Don't fan the flames.**
   Don't get self/others fired-up so that emotion clouds reason.

» **Don't be a gamer.**
   Don't try to convince self/others that it isn't wrong, "just how the game is played."

© 2016 Institute for Excellence & Ethics (IEE)   www.excellenceandethics.org

---

◊   *Conscience is an awareness of what is right or wrong with respect to our own conduct, intentions, and character; coupled with a sense of obligation to do what is right.*

◊ *Although we often think of conscience as rooted in our heart, one's conscience is actually rooted in the head, the heart, and the hands. It's not just **how** we feel; it's **what** we know, feel, and do regarding what is right and wrong.*

◊ *The Rules of an Active Conscience provides the strategies that will help defend our conscience and overcome the pressure to silence it, which can come from others or from within ourselves.*

It is important to clarify that the Rules of an Active Conscience work together in order to develop our thoughts, feelings, and actions in regards to right and wrong, but they should not serve as a way to hide acts of others that are wrong. For example, while we want students to learn that they should not always "play the victim," it is important for them to also know that if they feel like they are a victim in any situation, they should seek counsel from a trusted, responsible individual.

Guided Practice:

4. Introduce the Other-Study video about Lance Armstrong, the cancer survivor and American cyclist who won the Tour de France 7 times. Armstrong maintained throughout his string of victories that he never used banned substances to cheat and gain an unfair advantage. He later admitted to lying and in this video we get insights into his INactive Conscience.

   "Lance Armstrong: After the Apology"

   https://www.youtube.com/watch?v=KQDmX5nVbVw

5. As students observe the Other-Study, have them look for examples (stated or implied) of the Rules of an Active Conscience and how Armstrong justified or rationalized his lying and cheating (#1 in the Student Workbook).

6. Facilitate a discussion based on the evidence gathered by students from this Other-Study. Replicate the chart from the Student Workbook onto a chalk, white or smart board and fill in the evidence showing how Armstrong made his conscience INactive.

7. Now, have students work in small groups to complete the SHORT-TERM GAIN/LONG-TERM LOSS assessment in their workbooks. Introduction might sound something like this:

    ◊   *Whenever we do something that is wrong, unethical, or illegal we are usually doing so with hopes of gaining something that we want or believe we must have NOW, in the short-term. However, often it's the LONG-TERM LOSS that we fail to think about. As you think about the Lance Armstrong Other-Study, brainstorm what you believe he gained in the short term, and what you believe he lost in the long term.*

8. Facilitate a whole group discussion to try and determine short-term gain and long-term loss for Armstrong.

9. Introduce the second Other-Study about Tommie Smith and John Carlos, African American Olympic Athletes whose active conscience lead them to draw the world's attention to the injustices they perceived. As students observe the Other-Study instruct them to make notes in #3 in the Student Workbook about the examples of the power of conscience and courage in this Other-Study.

    "1968 Summer Olympics, Black Power Salute"

    https://www.youtube.com/watch?v=qck5arjMGBg

10. Facilitate a discussion on the role of conscience and courage in this Other-Study.

11. Following the discussion have students in small groups complete the SHORT-TERM LOSS/LONG-TERM GAIN assessment in #4 in the Student Workbook.

12. Debrief the small group discussion. Processing of this discussion might note or address the following:

    ◊   *Tommie Smith and John Carlos suffered greatly in the short term for following their conscience, but in the long term are viewed as true and lasting heroes, men of integrity and justice whose actions forever changed the world.*

    ◊   *Whereas, Lance Armstrong profited greatly in the short term, but in the long term will be remembered as a liar, a cheat, and a bully.*

◊ *Lance Armstrong's name will be forever synonymous with cheating; Tommie Smith and John Carlos will be forever remembered for justice.*

◊ *It's not always easy to do the right thing in the short term, but if we remain true to our conscience and our deepest values about right and wrong, we can hope to have a clear conscience and the rewards—internal and external—that come from standing up for what is right.*

13. As a whole class brainstorm a list of the most common examples where we are challenged to compromise our integrity or to ignore our conscience. Examples might include: cheating on tests or handing in work copied from internet or others, stealing clothing, electronics of other merchandise from stores; using performance enhancing drugs, stealing from the workplace, NOT helping someone in need or in danger, etc.

14. Once the list of examples has been created, identify the 3 or 4 most common (or most important). Have students work in small groups to 1) identify the Rules of an Active Conscience that are ignored in order to rationalize these behaviors, and 2) the potential long-term loss that could result from ignoring our conscience and engaging in these behaviors (#5 in the Student Workbook).

15. Debrief the small group discussions.

Closure & Assessment:

16. Close the lesson by discussing important considerations in developing an active conscience, and how the Rules of an Active Conscience can help. Closing remarks may sound something like this:

◊ *In order to develop an active conscience, it's important to consider what factors lead to a weak conscience. For example:*

» *Ignorance can lead to a weak conscience: you simply might not see or understand that there is an issue to be concerned about.*

» *Lack of experience is a factor: you might not have faced something like this before.*

» *Misinformation: you either might not have all the facts, or you could have the wrong facts.*

> » *Prejudicial attitudes: you could be subject, or you might subject others, to prejudice based on race, gender, or economic status.*

> ◊ *In order to develop and defend our conscience, we must overcome the pressure to silence it, which can come from others or from within ourselves. The strategies in the Rules of an Active Conscience can help you overcome this pressure.*

17. Have students identify, either privately or to share with a partner, group, etc., one area in which they could apply the knowledge presented in the Rules of an Active Conscience to begin making better decisions that will develop and defend their conscience (#6 in the Student Workbook).

Extension:

18. **Other-Study:** Search and study current examples of cheating in education, athletics, civic, government, and workplace. Study text or video from David Callahan and his work, *The Cheating Culture* (http://www.cheatingculture.com/). Study text or video on Dan Ariely's work, *The Honest Truth About Dishonesty* (for example, https://www.youtube.com/watch?v=XBmJay_qdNc).

19. **Self-Study:** Have students identify the Rule of an Active Conscience that they break most often in relation to the areas identified in this module. Using a plain white adhesive nametag, a blank 3x5 index card, half sheet of paper, etc., have each student draw a picture that reminds them of the way they commonly quiet their conscience (for example, a student identifying that they often allow emotion to cloud reason and therefore break the "don't fan the flames" rule, might draw a campfire). Then have each student affix their picture to the front cover of their student planner, or another place where they will see it regularly.

20. **Performance/Simulation:** Have students act out scenarios that represent each of the Rules of an Active Conscience, silent film style! Write each Rule of an Active Conscience on a slip of paper, then place the slips of paper into a hat, basket, etc. After placing students in groups, have a representative from each group draw a Rule. Give groups a stated amount of time to plan their skit, explaining to them that the skits must be performed with no voices! Encourage students to be creative, use props that are present in the room, etc. You might even choose to show video clips of some silent films in order to give them an idea of the way

actors performed in that medium. After groups have been given the chance to prepare, have 1 group at a time deliver their silent skit. At the conclusion of each skit, have students guess which Rule the performing group was portraying.

21. **Support & Challenge:** Prepare students to share the Rules of an Active Conscience with others by having them practice discussing it in scenarios they might encounter. Have students identify scenarios in which they have seen other students in their school, people outside of the school, or even themselves quiet their conscience (you may want to encourage anonymity). Have students brainstorm ways that they could discuss the Rules of an Active Conscience with the people in these scenarios in order to help them stop quieting their conscience and start building their integrity. Then have students think of ways that after initially discussing the Rules with someone, they could support that person moving forward in order to help them make better choices.

Planning and Reflection

Planning and Reflection

Module 6-2: Creating a Personal Character Touchstone

Competency: Develop an ethical code of conduct

Tools: *Personal Character Touchstone and Values Map*

⊘ EXCELLENCE WITH INTEGRITY

PERSONAL CHARACTER TOUCHSTONE TEMPLATE

Be your best self; live your best life today

by creating a motto:

» that expresses the moral and performance character values defining the core of your identity and guiding your behavior;

» that describes how you would like to be remembered.

Adaptability   Caring
Ambition   Civility   Citizenship
Craftsmanship   Confidence   Courage   Compassion
Critical Thinking   Collaboration   Cooperation   Courtesy
Dependability   Creativity   Emotional Intelligence
Diligence   Curiosi·   ɪpathy   Forgiveness
Drive   Determination   Friendliness   Graciousness
Effort   Entrepreneurship   Generosity   Gratitude
Enthusiasm   Endurance   Honesty   Honor   Hope
Grit Imagination   Initiative   Humility   Integrity
Passion   Justice   Loyalty   Kindness   Love
Perseverance Organizatioɪ   ɪoderation   Mercy
Positive Attitude Pride in Work   Patience   Peacefulness
Resilience   Resourcefulness   Responsibility   Respect
Self-Awareness   Thrift   Self-Control   Sensitivity
Service   Truthfulness   Trustworthiness
Work Ethic   Wisdom

Adapted from Lickona & Davidson (2005)

© 2016 Institute for Excellence & Ethics (IEE)   www.excellenceandethics.org

---

⊘ EXCELLENCE WITH INTEGRITY

VALUES MAP

Adaptability   Caring

Ambition   Civility   Citizenship

Craftsmanship   Confidence   Courage   Compassion

Critical Thinking   Collaboration   Cooperation   Courtesy

Dependability   Creativity   Emotional Intelligence

Diligence   Curiosi·   ɪpathy   Forgiveness

Drive   Determination   Friendliness   Graciousness

Effort   Entrepreneurship   Generosity   Gratitude

Enthusiasm   Endurance   Honesty   Honor   Hope

Grit Imagination   Initiative   Humility   Integrity

Passion   Justice   Loyalty   Kindness   Love

Perseverance Organizatioɪ   ɪoderation   Mercy

Positive Attitude Pride in Work   Patience   Peacefulness

Resilience   Resourcefulness   Responsibility   Respect

Self-Awareness   Thrift   Self-Control   Sensitivity

Service   Truthfulness   Trustworthiness

Work Ethic   Wisdom

Adapted from Lickona & Davidson (2005).

© 2016 Institute for Excellence & Ethics (IEE)   www.excellenceandethics.org

Objective

Students will use the Personal Character Touchstone activity to develop an ethical code of conduct.

Overview

1. Students will participate in an activity where they identify words or phrases that describe how a hero they admire lives/lived their life.

2. Students will view a video titled, "What's Your Sentence?" by Daniel Pink, as well as a video that contains responses to his question.

3. Students will create their own Personal Character Touchstone and share it in a video style format.

Preparation

1. Determine how you will establish the behavioral norms needed to ensure a positive and productive learning experience for all students.

2. Determine facilitation procedures and timing for the sharing of personal character touchstones.

3. Prepare external streaming video content:

    a. Review IEE policy regarding use of external content.

    b. "What's Your Sentence?" (prompt)

    http://vimeo.com/14888034.

    c. "What's Your Sentence?: The Video" (responses)

    http://vimeo.com/18347489.

    d. "What's My Sentence? 4th Hour"

    https://www.youtube.com/watch?v=aTEcZDJy81s.

Materials

*   Blank paper for each student.
*   Drawing supplies (markers, crayons, colored pencils, etc.).

Module Delivery Steps

Introduction:

1. Begin the lesson by displaying the following Abraham Lincoln quote, "*Whatever you are, be a good one,*" and asking students what they think Lincoln meant by it. Discussion should move toward an understanding among students that being true to who they are and being the best person they themselves can be is what is truly important.

2. Introduce the Personal Character Touchstone Template.

⊘ *EXCELLENCE WITH INTEGRITY*

PERSONAL CHARACTER TOUCHSTONE TEMPLATE

Be your best self; live your best life today

by creating a motto:

» **that expresses the moral and performance character values defining the core of your identity and guiding your behavior;**

» **that describes how you would like to be remembered.**

Adaptability Caring
Ambition Civility Citizenship
Craftsmanship Confidence Courage Compassion
Critical Thinking Collaboration Cooperation Courtesy
Dependability Creativity Emotional Intelligence
Diligence Curiosi... ...npathy Forgiveness
Drive Determination Friendliness Graciousness
Effort Entrepreneurship Generosity Gratitude
Enthusiasm Endurance Honesty Honor Hope
Grit Imagination Initiative Humility Integrity
Passion Justice Loyalty Kindness Love
Perseverance Organizatio... ...loderation Mercy
Positive Attitude Pride in Work Patience Peacefulness
Resilience Resourcefulness Responsibility Respect
Self-Awareness Thrift Self-Control Sensitivity
Service Truthfulness Trustworthiness
Work Ethic Wisdom

Adapted from Lickona & Davidson (2005).

 www.excellenceandethics.org

Introduction to the tool may sound something like this:

◊ *A character touchstone is a go-to ethical framework, or guide. It consists of a concise statement of core beliefs and the standards by which we guide our lives.*

3.   Introduce the activity in #1 in the Student Workbook, which asks for each student to identify a hero that they admire for the way they live (or lived) their life.

4.   Ask for volunteers to share their hero and the guidelines/rules they listed.

5.   Display the Values Map, and ask students to identify words from the Tool that correspond with what they wrote about their hero's guidelines or rules (or that they could add to a description of their hero). Explain to students that these character competencies are often what we are drawn to when we think of a "hero," and that the competencies are also things that we can work hard to strengthen in ourselves as well.

⊘ EXCELLENCE WITH INTEGRITY

VALUES MAP

Adaptability   Caring

Ambition   Civility   Citizenship

Craftsmanship   Confidence   Courage   Compassion

Critical Thinking   Collaboration   Cooperation   Courtesy

Dependability   Creativity   Emotional Intelligence

Diligence   Curiosit͟   ͟pathy   Forgiveness

Drive   Determination   Friendliness   Graciousness

Effort   Entrepreneurship   Generosity   Gratitude

Enthusiasm   Endurance   Honesty   Honor   Hope

Grit   Imagination   Initiative   Humility   Integrity

Passion   Justice   Loyalty   Kindness   Love

Perseverance   Organizatioi   ͟oderation   Mercy

Positive Attitude   Pride in Work   Patience   Peacefulness

Resilience   Resourcefulness   Responsibility   Respect

Self-Awareness   Thrift   Self-Control   Sensitivity

Service   Truthfulness   Trustworthiness

Work Ethic   Wisdom

Performance Character

Moral Character

Adapted from Lickona & Davidson (2005).

Guided Practice:

6. Continue the lesson by introducing the Personal Character Touchstone activity. In order to introduce the activity, display and discuss the Personal Character Touchstone Template, then show students the "What's Your Sentence?" video by Daniel Pink, followed by video(s) of responses people have submitted:

    ◊ *In his book, <u>Drive: The Surprising Truth About What Motivates Us</u> (Pink, 2009) author Daniel Pink describes an activity called "What's Your Sentence?" Let's take a look at him issuing a challenge for people to participate in an online video he posted in 2010:*

    "What's Your Sentence?"

    http://vimeo.com/14888034

    ◊ *This is the video Daniel Pink and Sophia Pink Films put together based on the responses they received.*

    "What's Your Sentence?: The Video"

    http://vimeo.com/18347489

    ◊ *The next video is a collection of responses from a high school class.*

    "What's My Sentence? 4th Hour"

    https://www.youtube.com/watch?v=aTEcZDJy81s

    Note: in this video, several students make references to their personal faith. Some students may feel it necessary to include reference to their personal beliefs when developing their own Personal Character Touchstone. For additional information related to this topic, see chapter VIII "Spiritual Person Engaged in Crafting a Life of Noble Purpose" in *Smart & Good High Schools: Integrating Excellence & Ethics for Success in School, Work, and Beyond* (Lickona & Davidson, 2005). This book is available for a free download in pdf format here:

    https://www2.cortland.edu/centers/character/high-schools/SnGReport.pdf.

7. Facilitate a discussion about the "What's Your Sentence?" response videos. Possible discussion prompts may be:

    ◊ *What moral and performance character traits did the responders include?*

    ◊ *Which sentences stood out for you? Why?*

8. Have students practice the "What's Your Sentence?" activity by writing a sentence for their hero (#2 in the Student Workbook).

9. Ask for volunteers to read their hero's sentence aloud to the group.

10. Have students begin the process of developing their own Personal Character Touchstone by selecting two performance character traits and two moral character traits that best align with the guidelines on the Personal Character Touchstone Template (#3 in the Student Workbook, Step 1).

11. When students have completed Step 1, move on to Step 2—using the identified character competencies to write a Personal Character Touchstone.

12. When all or most of the students have developed their sentence, pass out blank paper and drawing supplies (markers, crayons, colored pencils, etc.) and have students begin creating their Personal Character Touchstone. Encourage students to be creative and allow their entire paper, not just the actual words, to represent their Touchstone.

13. Facilitate a public presentation of the touchstones similar to the video format where each student simply holds up and reads his or her Personal Character Touchstone.

Closure & Assessment:

14. Close the lesson by explaining that the Personal Character Touchstones that were developed through this activity can help students guide their decisions. Have students reflect on how they will commit to using their touchstone (see some suggestions in #4 in the Student Workbook).

Extension:

15. **Other-Study:** Use the "FISH" Philosophy to examine how Pike Place Fish Company employees bring their touchstone to life every day:

    - Play
    - Make their day
    - Be there
    - Choose your attitude

    See the related video "SEATTLE PIKE PLACE FISH CO":

    https://www.youtube.com/watch?v=TbtsfyrEF_c

16. **Self-Study:** Personal Character Touchstones affect not only the lives of the individual students, but lives of those that they interact with. For example, the employees at the Pike Place Fish Market are not just trying to figure out how to sell people fish; they are out to discover how to make their day. Ask students to think about their Personal Character Touchstone and describe how by living their Touchstone to the fullest they can have a positive impact on the lives of others.

17. **Performance/Simulation:** Video your students holding and speaking their Personal Character Touchstones. This is a great way to incorporate multimedia literacy skills and creates an opportunity for you and your students to show off the cool things you are doing in your class.

18. **Support & Challenge:** Assign each student an accountability partner. Have students share their Personal Character Touchstones with each other, then write their partner's Touchstone in their planner or somewhere else they will be able to keep and see it often. Schedule regular check-in times when students can briefly meet with their partner to see if they are living out their Touchstone, if they need additional help and support to do so, or if their Touchstone needs to be revised. Encourage students to check in with their partners outside of the regular meeting times as well.

Planning and Reflection

Bibliography

Allison, J. & Gediman, D. (2006). *This I believe: The personal philosophies of remarkable men and women.* New York, NY: Holt.

Berger, R. (2003). *An ethic of excellence.* Portsmouth, NH: Heinemann.

Bethel, S. M. (1990). *Making a difference: Twelve qualities that make you a leader.* New York, NY: Berkley Books.

Blanchard, K., & Hodges, P. (2003). *The servant leader: Transforming your heart, head, hands and habits.* Nashville, TN: J. Countryman.

Bloom, B. (1985). *Developing talent in young people.* New York, NY: Ballantine Books.

Callahan, D. (2004). *The cheating culture: Why more Americans are doing wrong to get ahead.* New York, NY: Harcourt.

Callahan, S. (1991). *In good conscience: Reason and emotion in moral decision making.* San Francisco, CA: Harper.

Casner-Lotto, J., Rosenblum, E., & Wright, M. (2009). *The ill-prepared U.S. workforce: Exploring the challenges of employer-provided workforce readiness training.* New York, NY: The Conference Board, Inc.

Casner-Lotto, J., & Wright, M. (2006). *Are they really ready to work: Employers perspectives on the basic knowledge and applied skills of new entrants to the 21st century U.S. workforce.* New York, NY: The Conference Board, Inc.

Cherniss, C., & Goleman, D. (2001). *The emotionally intelligent workplace: How to select for, measure, and improve emotional intelligence in individuals, groups, and organizations.* San Francisco, CA: Jossey-Bass.

Collins, J. (2001). *Good to great: Why some companies make the leap and others don't.* New York, NY: Harper Collins.

Colvin, G. (2008). *Talent is overrated: what really separates world-class performers from everybody else.* New York, NY: Penguin.

Covey, S. R. (1990). *The seven habits of highly effective people.* New York, NY: Simon & Schuster.

Covey, S. R. (1991). *Principle-centered leadership.* New York, NY: Summit Books.

Covey, S. R. (1994). *First things first.* New York, NY: Fireside.

Covey, S. R. (2004). *The 8th habit: From effectiveness to greatness*. New York, NY: Free Press.

Crandall, D. (2007). *Leadership lessons from West Point*. New York, NY: Leader to Leader Institute.

Csikszentmihalyi, M. (1990). *Flow: The psychology of optimal experience*. New York, NY: Harper Collins Publishers.

Csikszentmihalyi, M., Ratunde, K., & Whalen, S. (1993). *Talented teenagers: The roots of success and failure*. New York, NY: Cambridge University Press.

Damon, W., Menon, J., & Bronk, K. C. (2003). The development of purpose during adolescence. *Applied Developmental Science*, 7, (2), 119-128.

Davidson, M. L. (2012). Creating an intentional culture of excellence in the workplace. *Journal of Dermatology for Physician Assistants*, 6(2), 53-54.

Davidson, M.L., Khmelkov, V.T., & Baker, K. (2011). Sustainability and enduring impact: Shaping an intentional culture of excellence and ethics. *Journal of Character and Leadership Integration*, 2:1, 35-51.

Drucker, P. F. (2007). *The effective executive*. Oxford: Butterworth-Heinemann.

Dweck, C.S. (2006). *Mindset: the new psychology of success*. New York, NY: Ballantine Books.

Ericsson, K. A., Charness, N., Feltovich, P. J., & Hoffman, R. R. (2006). *The Cambridge handbook of expertise and expert performance*. New York, NY: Cambridge University Press.

Fisher, R., Ury, W., & Patton, B. (1991). *Getting to yes: Negotiating agreement without giving in*. New York, NY: Penguin.

Frankl, V. E. (1984). *Man's search for meaning*. New York, NY: Washington Square Press.

Gardner, H. (1997). *Extraordinary minds: Portraits of 4 exceptional individuals and an examination of our own extraordinariness*. New York, NY: Basic Books.

Gardner, H. (2007). *Five minds for the future*. Boston, MA: Harvard Business School Press.

Gardner, H., Csikszentmihalyi, M., & Damon, B. (2001). *Good work: When excellence and ethics meet*. New York, NY: Basic Books.

Gawande, A. (2007). *Better: A surgeon's notes on performance.* New York, NY: Henry Holt and Company.

Gelb, M. J. (1998). *How to think like Leonardo da Vinci: Seven steps to genius every day.* New York, NY: Dell Publishing.

Ginott, H. G. (2003). *Between parent and child: The bestselling classic that revolutionized parent-child communication (Revised and updated).* New York, NY: Three Rivers Press.

Gladwell, M. (2005). *Blink: The power of thinking without thinking.* Boston: Little, Brown & Company.

Gladwell, M. (2008). *Outliers: The story of success.* New York, NY: Little, Brown & Company.

Goleman, D. (1995). *Emotional intelligence: Why it can matter more than IQ.* New York, NY: Bantam.

Heath, C., & Heath D. (2008). *Made to stick: Why some ideas survive and others die.* New York, NY: Random House.

Heath, C., & Heath D. (2010). *Switch: How to change things when change is hard.* New York, NY: Crown Publishing.

Johnson, S. (2010). *Where good ideas come from: The natural history of innovation.* New York, NY: Riverhead.

Kanter, R. M. (2004). *Confidence: How winning streaks & losing streaks begin and end.* New York, NY: Crown.

Kidder, R. M. (2005). *Moral courage.* New York, NY: Harper Collins.

Kotter, J. P., & Cohen, D. S. (2002). *The heart of change: Real-life stories of how people change their organizations.* Boston, MA: Harvard Business School Press.

Kouzes, J. M., & Posner, B. Z. (2007). *The leadership challenge: How to get extraordinary things done in organizations.* New York, NY: John Wiley & Sons, Inc.

Kushner, H. S. (2001). *Living a life that matters.* New York, NY: Anchor Book.

Lickona, T., & Davidson, M. (2005). *Smart & good high schools: Integrating excellence and ethics for success in school, work, and beyond.* Cortland, NY: Center for the 4th and 5th Rs.

Lehrer, J. (2012). *Imagine: how creativity works.* New York, NY: Houghton Mifflin Harcourt Publishing Company.

Loehr, J. & Schwartz, T. (2003). *The power of full engagement: Managing energy, not time, is the key to high performance and personal renewal.* New York, NY: Free Press.

Lovat, T., Toomey, R., & Clement, N. (2010). *International research handbook on values education and student wellbeing.* New York, NY: Springer.

Marriner, M., Gebhard, N., & Gordon, J. (2006). *Roadtrip nation: A guide to discovering your path in life. A handbook of creative-thinking techniques.* New York, NY: Ballantine Books.

Maxwell, J. C. & Dornan, J. (1997). *Becoming a person of influence: How to positively impact the lives of others.* Nashville, TN: Thomas Nelson Publishers.

Maxwell, J. C. (2007). *The 21 irrefutable laws of leadership: Follow them and people will follow you.* Nashville, TN: Thomas Nelson Publishers.

Michalko, M. (2006). *Thinkertoys: A handbook of creative-thinking techniques.* New York, NY: Ten Speed Press.

Molden, D., & Dweck, C. (2000). Meaning and motivation. In C. Sansone & J. M. Harackiewicz (Eds.), *Intrinsic and extrinsic motivation: The search for optimal motivation and performance* (pp. 131-153). New York, NY: Academic Press.

Motimer, J.T. (2003). *Working and growing up in America.* Cambridge, MA: Harvard University Press.

Nicholls, J.G. (1983). Conceptions of ability and achievement motivation: A theory and its implications for education. In S.G. Paris, G.M. Olson, & H.W. Stevenson (Eds.), *Learning and motivation in the classroom.* Hillsdale, NJ: Lawrence Erlbaum Associates.

Nuwer, H. (2002). *Wrongs of passage: Fraternities, sororities, hazing and binge drinking.* Indiana: Indiana University Press.

Oliner, S. P., & Oliner,M. P. (1988). *The altruistic personality: Rescuers of Jews in Nazi Europe.* New York, NY: Free Press.

Palermo, R.C. (2003). *Do the right things... right. It is that simple. A step-by-step guide to world-class performance.* New York, NY: The Strategic Triangle, Inc.

Peterson, C., & Seligman, M. (2004). *Character strengths and virtues: A handbook and classification.* Oxford: Oxford University Press.

Pink, D. H. (2005). *A whole new mind: Why right-brainers will rule the future*. New York, NY: Penguin Group.

Pink, D. H. (2009). *Drive: The surprising truth about what motivates us*. New York, NY: Penguin Group.

Pope, D. (2001). *"Doing school": how we are creating a generation of stressed out, materialistic, and miseducated students*. New Haven, CT: Yale University Press.

Putnam, R. (2000). *Bowling alone: The collapse and revival of American community*. New York, NY: Simon & Schuster.

Resnick, M. D., Bearman, P. S., Blum, R. W., et al. (1997). Protecting adolescents from harm: Findings from the National Longitudinal Study on Adolescent Health. *JAMA*, 278, 823-832.

Ritchhart, R. (2002). *Intellectual character: What it is, why it matters, and how to get it*. San Francisco, CA: Jossey Bass.

Scheider, B. & Stevenson, D. (2000). *The ambitious generation: America's teenagers, motivated but directionless*. New Haven, CT: Yale University Press.

Schwartz, T. (2010). *Be excellent at anything: The four keys to transforming the way we work and live*. New York, NY: Free Press.

Selye, H. (1975). *Stress without distress*. New York, NY: Signet.

Selye, H. (1978). *Stress of life*. New York, NY: McGraw Hill.

Senge, P. M. (1990). *The fifth discipline: The art and practice of the learning organization*. New York, NY: Currency.

Shinseki, E. K. (2004). *Be · know · do: Leadership the army way*. San Francisco, CA: Jossey-Bass.

Sternberg, R. J. (2007). *Successful intelligence: How practical and creative intelligence determine success in life*. New York, NY: Plume.

Sternberg, R. J., & Grigorenko, E. L. (2004). *Culture and competence: Contexts of life success*. Washington, DC: American Psychological Association.

Stoltz, P. G., & Weihemnmayer, E. (2006). *The adversity advantage: Turning everyday struggles into everyday greatness*. New York, NY: Fireside.

Terman, L. M. (1954). The discovery and encouragement of exceptional talent. *American Psychologist*, 9, 221-230.

Thaler, R. H. & Sunstein, C. R. (2009). *Nudge: Improving decisions about health, wealth, and happiness.* New York, NY: Penguin.

The Conference Board, Corporate Voices for Working Families, Partnership for 21st Century Skills, Society for Human Resource Management. (2006). *Are They Really Ready to Work? Employers' Perspectives on the Basic Knowledge and Applied Skills of New Entrants to the 21st Century U.S. Workforce.* Retrieved from http://www.p21.org/storage/documents/FINAL_REPORT_PDF09-29-06.pdf. Printed in USA. ISBN: No. 0-8237-0888-8.

Zins, J. E., Weissburg, R. P., Wang, M. C., & Walber, H. J. (2004). *Building academic success on social and emotional learning: What does the research say?* New York, NY: Teachers College Press.